You are my
Grammar &
Speaking

3 Student Book

I am books

Published by

I am Books

#1116, Daeryung Techno Town 12th Bldg.,

14, Gasan digital 2-ro, Geumcheon-gu, Seoul 153-778, Republic of Korea

TEL: 82-2-6343-0999

FAX: 82-2-6343-0995

Visit our website: http://www.iambooks.co.kr

Publishers: Shin Sunghyun, Oh Sangwook

Author: Lucifer EX

Editor: Lee Doohee

Photo Credits:

Wikipedia (www.wikipedia.org): p. 8 (Big Bang) © YG Entertainment; p. 36 (starved girl); p. 65 (1998-2005 Volkswagen New Beetle photographed in USA); p. 66 (Harry Potter British Books) © Mo HH92 (Original uploader at en.wikipedia); p. 67 (Mona Lisa); p. 104 (Bill Gates) © www.dts-nachrichtenagentur.de; p. 104 (Barack Obama); p. 110 (Kim Yuna) © Sfcphoto.KeunHwa; p. 112 (Korean Food "Bulgogi") © nate steiner (a flickr user); p. 126 (The Statue of Lee Sunshin)

Flickr (www.flickr.com): p. 62 (William Shakespeare) © CircaSassy; p. 68 ("CPS Students Practice Earthquake Drills on New Madrid Anniversary") © KOMUnews; p. 77 (No dogs sign) © ell brown; p. 79 (camping food) © iwona_kellie; p. 82 ("Korean Food") © L. Cheryl; p. 85 (fast food) © SteFou!; p. 85 (shopping in Dongdaemun) © USAG-Humphreys; p. 85 ("Best of Broadway 2011-2012 Series") © North Charleston; p. 85 (Namdaemun) © Charles Chan; p. 104 (Avatar) © tsmall; p. 104 (Harry Potter and the Chamber of Secrets) © Colin ZHU; p. 104 (Avatar iPhone Wallpaper) © xploitme; p. 104 (Matrix) © Chesi - Fotos CC; p. 111 (Blue Whale) © mikebaird; p. 117 ("Martineau Place - Pizza Hut") © ell brown;

All other photos © imagetoday (www.imagetoday.co.kr)

ISBN: 978-89-6398-095-9 63740

Preface

You are my Grammar & Speaking series is a basic grammar book for beginner learners. There are 61 units in series and each unit is about a different point of English grammar. With the various exercises, interesting photos, and illustrations, students will enjoy English grammar and really can communicate in English, even from the beginning. This book encourages students to speak and write English accurately and fluently by providing them with a solid understanding of English grammar.

This book uses a simple but systematic 4-step approach (Real-life Context, Learn & Practice, Super Writing, Super Speaking) to help young learners master English grammar. This series aims to motivate young learners to learn grammar through various creative tasks such as Super Writing, Super Speaking, and various levels of challenging questions.

You are my Grammar & Speaking series is a useful supplement to any English language courses and is suitable for both classroom teaching and self-study. The series focuses on the key grammar concepts that students need to know for written exercises.

I hope many students will build language and communication skills with this *You are my Grammar & Speaking series*. At the same time, I wish teachers will use *You are my Grammar & Speaking series* as the most appropriate tool for teaching English as a second language. If students learn one language well, they will be able to learn other languages easily. That is why grammar is necessary to learn languages.

I am convinced that through this *You are my Grammar & Speaking series*, a lot of students will definitely have the chance to improve and develop their English grammar skills and abilities.

Thanks and good luck,

Lucifer EX

Structure & Features

You are my Grammar & Speaking series is an easy, friendly, and interesting grammar book series designed for young learners. The series contains interesting photos and illustrations to help students understand grammar points. With this grammar book series, the leaners will learn the rules of essential English grammar with the information about when and how to use them.

• Step 1: *Real-life Context*

The purpose of this part is to introduce students to the grammar point of the unit. This helps students to start the lesson in a very meaningful real-life context with captivating images.

• Step 2: *Learn & Practice*

Vivid photos and illustrations stimulate students' interest and help them understand the meaning and use of grammar. Clear and easy-to-read grammar charts present the grammar structure. The accompanying examples ensure that students understand the grammar point with colorful photos and illustrations.

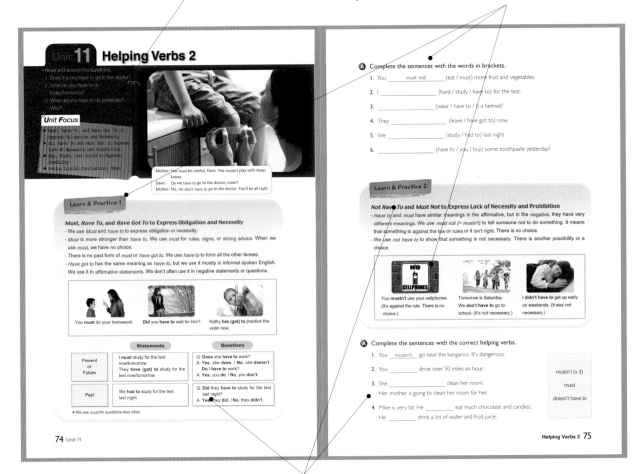

Each Learn & Practice provides various basic exercises and opportunities to practice both the forms and the uses of the grammar structure.

• Step 3: Super Writing

A writing activity allows students to interact with one another and further develop their speaking and writing skills. Through these activities, students will have a chance to apply their understanding of the practical uses of grammar.

• Step 4: Super Speaking

Super Speaking offers students rich opportunities to apply newly learned grammar to speaking activities. This section will help students to develop speaking skills. Students work in pairs or groups and perform a variety of real-life tasks, progressing smoothly from controlled to free practice. By doing so, the amount of time students speak is increased significantly and cooperation among students is encouraged. In addition, pair and group works help students lessen their communicative stress because it is easier for them to communicate with their peers rather than their teachers.

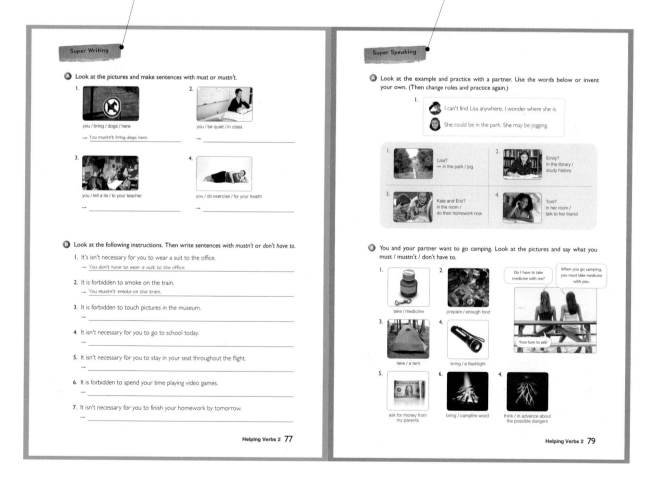

Contents

You are my
Grammar &
Speaking

3 Student Book

Simple Pesent vs. Present Progressive

- Read and answer the questions.
1. What is Julie doing now?
2. What is David doing tonight?
3. Do you enjoy listening to K-pop music?

Unit Focus

▶ Simple Present vs. Present Progressive
▶ Non-Progressive Verbs
▶ Present Progressive as a Future Tense

David: Julie, hi, it's David. Where are you now?
Julie: I'm at home. I'm playing the guitar with my father. What's up?
David: Well, I'm not playing soccer tonight. I'm going to Big Bang's concert.
Jane: Oh, really? I love Big Bang.
David: I know! I love them, too. They're giving a concert at Wembley Arena in London. What do you think?
Jane: Wow, I envy you. I really want to go there.

Learn & Practice 1

Simple Present vs. Present Progressive

The Present Simple	The Present Progressive

- Repeated actions or habits
  E.g. She **wakes up** every morning at 7:00.
 	
- General statements of fact or always true
  E.g. I usually **read** the newspaper in the morning.
  Water **boils** at 100 degrees Celsius.
	- For actions that are happening now, at the moment of speaking
	  E.g. It **isn't snowing** right now.
	
	- Around now
	  E.g. The earth **is becoming** warmer and warmer.
	
	- Future arrangements and plans
	  E.g. We**'re having** a party next week.

Time Expressions	**(Time) Expressions**
every morning/day/week/year, etc. on Monday/Tuesday, etc. in the morning/afternoon/evening always, never, sometimes, often, etc.	now, at the moment, at present, these days, this week/month/year, today, etc. Look!, Listen!

Ⓐ **Complete the sentences by using the words in brackets. Use the simple present or the present progressive.**

1. Anna ___studies___ (study) every evening.

2. Water _____ (freeze) at zero degrees Celsius.

3. Right now I'm in class. I _____ (sit) at my desk. I usually _____ (sit) at the same desk in class every day.

Non–Progressive Verbs

- We do not usually use some verbs in the Present Progressive. We call these non-progressive verbs.

She **loves** apple juice.
Olivia **wants** an apple.
She **is thinking** about eating one now.

Sense	Feeling	Knowledge
hear	enjoy	think
	feel	know
see	hate	
	want	believe
smell	like	
	love	understand
taste	need	remember

- Some verbs can be used in both the progressive and the non-progressive form.

Non-Action Verb ——————————— **Action in Progress**

The pizza **tastes** good.   I **am tasting** the pizza.

He **looks** angry.   What **are** you **looking** at?

She **has** a puppy.   They **are having** lunch.
I **think** she is happy.   The boy **is thinking** about eating cookies.

Ⓐ Circle the correct words and check the correct boxes.

	Non-Action	Action
1. Kelly (has / is having) two daughters.	✓	☐
2. The chef (is tasting / tastes) the soup now.	☐	☐
3. These flowers (are smelling / smell) good.	☐	☐
4. She (is looking / look) at us. Who is she?	☐	☐
5. Tom (has / is having) dinner right now.	☐	☐
6. I (am knowing / know) what you said.	☐	☐

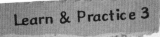

Present Progressive as a Future Tense

- The present progressive is used for future meaning when we are talking about plans that have already been made. We often use a time expression with the present progressive.
- We use the present progressive especially with verbs of movement and transportation such as come, go, leave, fly, and travel.

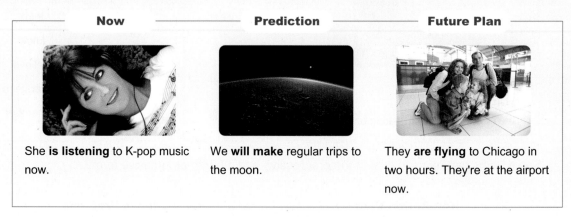

Now	**Prediction**	**Future Plan**
She **is listening** to K-pop music now.	We **will make** regular trips to the moon.	They **are flying** to Chicago in two hours. They're at the airport now.

- However, we cannot use the present progressive for future predictions.

A Are the following sentences present or future? Write *present* or *future* after each one.

1. My favorite TV program is starting in a minute. → <u>   future   </u>

2. He is seeing the director at 09:00 this morning. → _____

3. He's having dinner with some friends. → _____

4. I'm waiting for a call at the moment. → _____

5. My parents are coming to stay with me this weekend. → _____

6. I'm going shopping for some new clothes. → _____

7. Please be quiet or close the door. I'm speaking on the phone. → _____

8. She is writing an essay in her room. → _____

9. What time is Jacob arriving in Seoul? → _____

A Look at the pictures. Read the questions and answer them using the present simple or the present progressive.

1.

drink / orange juice

Q: What is he doing now?

A: *He is drinking orange juice.*

2.

go / to the concert

Q: What are they doing this Saturday?

A: _____

3.

play / chess

Q: What are Tom and Jane doing this evening?

A: _____

4.

eat / toast and jam / usually

Q: What does Karen usually eat for breakfast?

A: _____

B Complete the conversation using the information in the schedule. Use verbs in the present progressive and add any other words you need.

1. A: What _____*are you doing*_____ (you / do) on
   Monday night?
   B: _____*I'm going to the movie theater*_____ (I / go).

2. A: Who _____ (you / go) with?
   B: _____ (I / go).

Monday	9 p.m. - Movie theater - Olivia
Tuesday	
Wednesday	the Italian restaurant
Thursday	Meet Brian - the airport - 8:00
Friday	
Saturday	Brian - for weekend
Sunday	

3. A: What time _____ (you / meet) her?
   B: At _____.

4. A: And what about Wednesday? _____ (you / go out)?
   B: Yes, _____. _____ (I / go).

5. A: And Thursday?
   B: I _____ (meet).

6. A: What time _____ (he / arrive)?
   B: At _____.

C Read the sentences. Decide whether the verbs on the line are *RIGHT* or *WRONG*. Correct the verbs that are wrong.

1. I don't know her telephone number. → _____ RIGHT _____

   → _____

2. Please don't make so much noise. I study. → _____ WRONG _____

   → *Please don't make so much noise. I am studying.* _____

3. Look! Somebody is climbing that tree over there. → _____

   → _____

4. Can you hear those people? What do they talk about? → _____

   → _____

5. Are you believing in God? → _____

   → _____

6. The government is worried because the number of people without jobs increases.

   → _____

   → _____

D Complete the sentences with the words in parentheses. Use the simple present or the present progressive.

1. A: Be quiet! I ___ am listening ___ (listen) to the TV news.

   B: I ___ don't like ___ (not like) listening to the TV news.

2. We usually _____ (have) dinner in the kitchen, but this evening we are _____ (have) dinner in the garden because the weather is very warm.

3. A: _____ (you / smell) something funny?

   B: Yes, there is a lot of trash outside. Look!
      Your dog _____ (smell) it.

4. A: What _____ (you / think) about right now?

   B: I _____ (think) about snails.

   A: _____ (you / like) snails?

   B: Yes, I _____ (think) snails are interesting animals.

A Look at the example and practice with a partner. Use the words below or invent your own. (Then change roles and practice again.)

I.

1.

Olivia / every Monday → play tennis
this Saturday → watch a movie on TV

 What does Olivia do every Monday?

 She plays tennis.

 What is she doing this Saturday?

 She is watching a movie on TV.

2.

Alice / every Tuesday → go shopping
this Friday → work in her office

3.

Jessica / every morning → read a newspaper
tomorrow morning → jog in the park

4.

Tom / every evening → watch TV
tomorrow evening → ride a skateboard

5.

Peter and Shannon / every Saturday → study Korean
this Saturday → go to the movie theater

B Work with a partner. Ask each other about your plans. Use the present progressive as in the example.

Questions

1. what / do / after school?
2. what / do / tonight?
3. where / go / after school?
4. what / do / this weekend?
5. what / do / tomorrow?
6. when / go to bed / tonight?
7. what time / get up / tomorrow?
8. what / do / this Friday / Saturday/Sunday?

What are you doing after school?

I'm meeting Billy at 6:30.

Your turn now!

Unit **2** Simple Present vs. Simple Past

- Read and answer the questions.
1. Have you ever been to Dokdo?
2. Do you know the position of Dokdo?
3. Why does Japan say Dokdo is Japan's territory?

Unit Focus

▶ Simple Present vs. Simple Past
▶ Future: Simple Present
▶ *Used To*: Past Habits

There is a very beautiful island near Ulleung Island. It is Dokdo. Recently, Japan made many Koreans angry. They said Dokdo is their island. People all over the world know that Dokdo is in Korean territory. But Japan keeps saying it is theirs. They are even planning to teach their students the wrong history. They always want to take Dokdo away from Korea. However, Japan must stop doing such a stupid thing! And they have to apologize to Korea as soon as possible. Also, they have to let the whole world know that Dokdo is Korean territory.

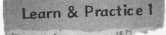
Learn & Practice 1

Simple Present vs. Simple Past

- We use the simple present to talk about habitual actions, and for things that happen all the time or are always true.
- We use the simple past to talk about actions and situations that began and ended in the past.
- In the simple present, we usually add *-s, -es,* or *-ies* to the base verb for he, she, it.
- To form the Simple Past of regular verbs, we add -ed or -d to the base form of the verb.

Ciara **walks** to school.
She **walked** to school.
She **doesn't** walk to school.
She **didn't** walk to school.

Q: **Does** Tom wash the car every day?
A: **Yes**, he **does**.
Q: **Did** he wash the car yesterday?
A: **No**, he **didn't**.

Questions			Answers	
Does	he/she/it	swim?	Yes, he/she/it does.	No, he/she/it doesn't.
Do	you/we/they/I	swim?	Yes, I/we/they do.	No, I/we/they don't.
Did	I/we/they/you he/she/it	swim?	Yes, I/we... did.	No, I/we... didn't.

A Circle the correct words and make *yes/no* questions.

1. She (cleans /(cleaned)) her room last night. → *Did she clean her room last night?*

2. I (listen / listened) to the radio every morning. → _____

3. He (saw / sees) new movies every week. → _____

4. It (snowed / snows) a lot in the winter in Korea. → _____

5. The Korean War (broke / breaks) out in 1950. → _____

6. We (eat / ate) dinner at a family restaurant last night. → _____

7. Water (freezes / froze) at zero degrees Celsius. → _____

Learn & Practice 2

Future: Simple Present

- The simple present can express future time when events are on a definite schedule or timetable.
Only a few verbs are used in the simple present to express future time. The most common are
arrive, leave, start, begin, end, close, open, finish, and be.

There **is** a meeting at 9:00 tomorrow morning.

My new job **starts** next week.

My train **leaves** at 7:00 tomorrow morning.

A Complete the sentences by using the words in brackets. Use the simple present or the present progressive.

1. The soccer game _____*begins*_____ (begin) at 5:00 tomorrow.

2. He _____ (play) tennis on Monday afternoon.

3. She _____ (go) to the dentist on Tuesday morning.

4. My train _____ (leave) at 11:30, so I need to be at the station by 11:15.

5. What time does the movie _____ (begin) this evening?

6. Ann _____ (fly) to Singapore next week.

7. The bus _____ (arrive) at three o'clock.

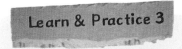
Used To: Past Habits

- *Used to* is past tense. We use it to talk about past habits or things that no longer exist at present. It has the same form in all persons, singular and plural.
- We form questions and negations with the helping verb *did / did not (= didn't)*, the subject and the verb *use* without -d.

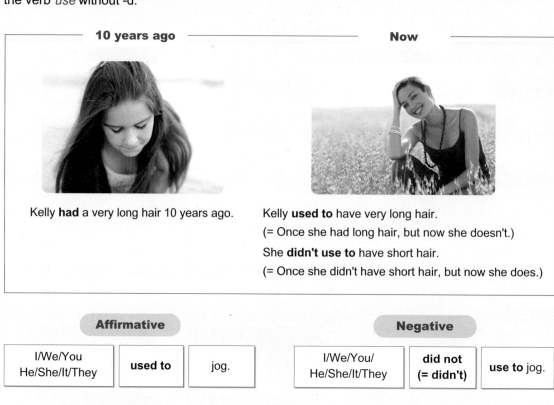

10 years ago	Now
Kelly **had** a very long hair 10 years ago.	Kelly **used to** have very long hair. (= Once she had long hair, but now she doesn't.) She **didn't use to** have short hair. (= Once she didn't have short hair, but now she does.)

Affirmative

I/We/You He/She/It/They	**used to**	jog.

Negative

I/We/You/ He/She/It/They	**did not** (= **didn't**)	use to jog.

Question

Did	I/We/You He/She/It/They	**use to**	jog?

Q: **Did** she **use to** play the guitar?
A: **Yes**, she **did**. / **No**, she **didn't**.

Ⓐ Complete the sentences with the correct form of *used to* and the verbs in brackets.

1. He ___*didn't use to eat*___ (not / eat) junk food.

2. She _____ (brush) her teeth after every meal, but now she brushes them in the evening only.

3. John _____ (go) shopping every day when he was rich.

4. Did you _____ (ride) a bicycle?

5. They _____ (not / eat) breakfast.

A Look at the pictures and prompts. Write questions and answers using the simple present or the simple past.

1.
Now

Rachel / go rollerblading / ?
No → take a tennis lesson

Q: Does Rachel go rollerblading?

A: No, she doesn't. She takes a tennis lesson.

2.
last weekend

Cindy / play the cello / ?
No → study Korean

Q: _____

A: _____

3.
Now

Tara / watch a DVD / ?
No → listen to K-pop music

Q: _____

A: _____

4.
last weekend

Aiden / go to the movies with his friends / ?
No → visit London

Q: _____

A: _____

5.
last weekend

Eric and Susan / go to a ballpark to watch a baseball game / ?
No → watch a soccer game on TV

Q: _____

A: _____

B Write six sentences about what you used to do when you were a child.

1. I used to wear glasses when I was a child.

2. _____

3. _____

4. _____

5. _____

6. _____

C Write sentences about Isabella and William. Use *used to* and *didn't use to*.

Isabella Now	Isabella Past		William Now	William Past
√	X	ride a bicycle to school	X	√
X	√	play badminton after school	√	X
√	X	eat lunch at the cafeteria	X	√
X	√	read history books	√	X

Isabella

William

1. Isabella didn't use to ride a bicycle to school, but she does now.
2. William used to ride a bicycle to school, but he doesn't now.
3. _____
4. _____
5. _____
6. _____
7. _____
8. _____

D Look at the pictures and prompts. Write questions and answers as in the example.

1.

Q: What time does your plane leave tomorrow?
A: My plane (= It) leaves at 8:00 tomorrow.

your plane / leave / tomorrow / ?
→ 8:00

2.

Q: _____
A: _____

the baseball game / begin / tomorrow / ?
→ 5:00

3.

Q: _____
A: _____

the laundry shop / open / tomorrow / ?
→ 9:00

A Look at the example and practice with a partner. Use the words below or invent your own. (Then change roles and practice again.)

I.

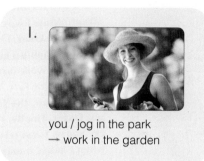

I.
you / jog in the park
→ work in the garden

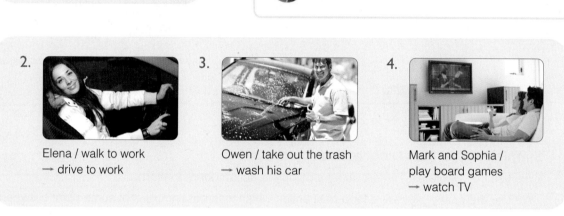

What do you usually do in the morning?

I usually jog in the park.

What did you do this morning?

I worked in the garden.

2.

Elena / walk to work
→ drive to work

3.

Owen / take out the trash
→ wash his car

4.
Mark and Sophia /
play board games
→ watch TV

B Work with a partner. Look at the pictures and say what Mike used to do and what he does now.

Now
live in / a big house

Last Year
live in / a small house

Did Mike use to live in a big house?

No, he didn't. He used to live in a small house, but now he lives in a big house.

Now
go to work / by car

Last Year
go to work / by bus

You turn to ask now!

Now
eat breakfast /
in a restaurant

Last Year
eat breakfast /
at home

Now
spend / his holidays /
traveling the world

Last Year
spend / his holidays /
at a campsite

Unit 3 Simple Past vs. Past Progressive

• Read and answer the questions.
1. Why was the woman walking fast?
2. What did she leave on the bus?
3. If you hear footsteps behind you at night, what do you do?

It was a night. There was a full moon with a few dark clouds drifting over it. When I **got off** the bus, there was no one in the street. While I **was walking** down the street, I **heard** footsteps behind me. When I **began** to walk fast, the footsteps **got** fast. When I **began** to run, the footsteps **got** faster. Finally, I **got** to my house. I **was screaming** when I **heard** a man's voice behind me, "Is this your smartphone? You **left** it on the bus."

Unit Focus

▶ Simple Past vs. Past Progressive
▶ Past Progressive: Time Clauses with *While* and *When*
▶ Simple Past: Time Clauses with *When, Before, After,* and *As Soon As*

Learn & Practice 1

Simple Past vs. Past Progressive

- We use the *simple past* to talk about a complete action (long or short).
- We use the past progressive for a past action which was not complete at some point between its beginning and end.

Simple Past	Past Progressive

I **called** you lots of times, but you **didn't answer** the phone.	Susan and Tom **were sleeping** at 10:00 yesterday.

Ⓐ Read and circle the correct words.

1. Cindy (played / was playing) badminton yesterday.

2. Megan and Seth (helped / were helping) their mother with the housework last night.

3. What were you (did / doing) at 11:00 yesterday?

4. Christopher Columbus (arrived / was arriving) in America in 1492.

5. A: Where were you going when I saw you yesterday?
   B: I (was going / went) to the post office.

Past Progressive: Time Clauses with While and When

- We often use the past progressive and the simple past together in a sentence. The past pogressive describes the longer action that was in progress in the past; the simple past describes the shorter action that happened (began and finished) in the middle of the longer action.

- A time clause alone is not complete sentence. We must connect it to a main clause to form a complete sentence.

While Cory **was walking** to school this morning, it **began** to rain.

Cory **was walking** to school. (longer action)
It **began** to rain. (shorter action)

Time Clause

> **When** the phone **rang,**
> **While** she **was driving,**

Main Clause

> I **was sleeping**.
> a blind man **crossed** the street.

Main Clause

> I **was sleeping**
> A blind man **crossed** the street

Time Clause

> **when** the phone **rang**.
> **while** she **was driving**.

Ⓐ Complete the sentences with the *simple past* or the *past progressive* of the verbs shown on the pictures.

1.
   EAT
   COME

2.
   SEE
   RIDE

3.
   ARRIVE
   PLAY

4.
   GO
   BRUSH

5.
   EXPLAIN
   FALL

6.
   FIND
   READ

1. He ___was eating___ an apple when his teacher ___came___ in.

2. Peter _____ his bicycle when I _____ him yesterday.

3. The child _____ computer games when his mother _____.

4. The light _____ out while Paul _____ his teeth.

5. While the teacher _____ the lesson, he _____ asleep.

6. While she _____ the book, she _____ an unknown word.

Simple Past: Time Clauses with *When, Before, After,* and *As Soon As*

- We use the simple [ast to show that one action immediately followed another action.
- A time clause alone is not a complete sentence. We must use it with a main clauses to form a complete sentence.
- When two actions are in progress at the same time, we can use the *Past Progressive* in both parts of the sentence.

When the phone **rang**, I **answered** it.
First: The phone rang.
Then: I answered it.

While I **was reading** a newspaper, my husband **was writing** an email.

Main Clause	Time Clause
After I **finished** my homework, **As soon as** she **finished** her work,	I **went** to a movie. she **went** to bed.

Main Clause	Time Clause
I **went** to a movie She **went** to bed	**after** I **finished** my homework. **as soon as** she **finished** her work.

A Combine the two sentences in any order, using the time expression in parentheses.

1. They looked both ways. They crossed the street. (before)
   → They looked both ways before they crossed the street.
   → Before they crossed the street, they looked both ways.

2. We were very surprised. We heard the news. (when)
   → _____
   → _____

3. They started to dance. The music began. (as soon as)
   → _____
   → _____

A Change the simple past sentences to past progressive sentences.

1. Olivia read a magazine in class yesterday.

   → Olivia was reading a magazine in class yesterday.

2. Louis turned the corner when I saw him.

   → _____

3. Dana watched a movie with her father.

   → _____

4. While she drove home, she listened to her car radio.

   → _____

5. The young mothers held their babies at the doctor's office.

   → _____

6. The girls had breakfast at the fast food restaurant this morning.

   → _____

B Look at the pictures. Ask the questions using the information in brackets and answer them.

1. (when / you / see her / yesterday)

   Q: What was Sarah doing when you saw her yesterday?

   A: She was listening to K-pop music when I saw her yesterday.

   Sarah / listen to K-pop music

2. (when / you / see them)

   Q: _____

   A: _____

   Katy and Logan / jog

3. (when / you / come home / from school)

   Q: _____

   A: _____

   your parents / watch TV

4. (when / you / come home / yesterday)

   Q: _____

   A: _____

   Amanda / wash her face

C Combine the two sentences into one sentence by using time clauses.

1.
after

First: They got home.
Then: They washed the car.

After they got home, they washed the car.

They washed the car after they got home.

2.
as soon as

First: The phone rang.
Then: I answered the phone.

_____

_____

3.
while

First: I was standing here.
Then: The accident occurred.

_____

_____

4.
when

First: It began to rain.
Then: We opened our umbrellas.

_____

_____

D Look at the information about Jason and Jennifer. Then complete the sentences about them using the past progressive or the simple past.

Jason

Jennifer

	Jason		Jennifer
1995~2000	lived in Seattle	1996	arrived in Seoul
2000~2001	took TESOL program	1996~2004	lived in Seoul
2001~2002	lived and worked in Seoul	1996~2000	studied at a university
2002~2005	taught English in an elementary school	2000~2008	worked for the company
2002	met Jennifer	2002	met Jason
2007	married Jennifer	2007	married Jason

1. In 1995, Jason _____was living_____ in Seattle.

2. When Jennifer _____ in Seoul in 1996, Jason _____ in Seattle.

3. From 1996 to 2000, Jennifer _____ at a university in Seoul.

4. In 2001, Jason _____ in Seoul, and he _____ there, too.

5. In 2002, Jennifer _____ Jason.

6. Jennifer _____ in Seoul when she _____ Jason.

7. In 2004, Jason _____ English in an elementary school.

8. Jason _____ English when he _____ Jennifer.

9. Jason married Jennifer while she _____ for the company.

A Look at the example and practice with a partner. Use the words below or invent your own. (Then change roles and practice again.)

1.

Julie → exercise

1.

 What was Julie doing when the fire broke out?

 She was exercising when the fire broke out.

2.

the girls
→ do some shopping

3.

the children → sleep

4.

Lillian → talk on the phone

5.

the directors → have a meeting

6.

Mary
→ work on the computer

7.

Sue and Jim
→ check some reports

B Work with a partner. Combine the two ideas into one sentence by using *before* and *after* to introduce time clauses. Make four sentences for each item.

1. I locked the door. I turned off the lights.
2. She watched a scary movie. She went to bed.
3. We bought tickets. We entered the movie theater.
4. They finished their work. They took a walk.
5. He arrived at the airport. The plane landed.
6. The children got home from school. They played computer games.

A: Before I turned off the lights, I locked the door.
B: I locked the door before I turned off the lights.
A: After I locked the door, I turned off the lights.
B: I turned off the lights after I locked the door.

Simple Past vs. Past Progressive 25

The Future Tense

- Read and answer the questions.
1. Is Ava going to have a party?
2. What is Ava going to do before she goes to the restaurant?
3. What will you do if the weather is nice tomorrow?

Unit Focus

▶ Future: *Be Going To / Will / Be About To*

▶ Future Conditional Sentences

▶ Future time clauses with when, before, and after

Ava: It's my birthday soon. I'll be twenty next Saturday.
Prince: Oh, really? Are you going to have a party?
Ava: I'm going to have a meal in a restaurant with a few friends if the weather is nice. Before we go to the restaurant, we're going to go to the amusement park.
Prince: That'll be very nice.

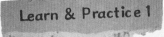

Learn & Practice 1

Future: Be Going To / Will / Be About To

- We use *will* + base verb for the future to make predictions about what we think will happen. We also use *will* for the future when we decide to do something at the time of speaking.
- We use *be going to* for plans and intentions for the (near) future. We also use *be going to* when there is evidence that something is going to happen in the near future.
- We use *be about to* + base verb to talk about an activity that will happen in the very near future, usually within minutes or seconds.

They **aren't going to** travel next week.

Kevin **is going to** fall. (There is visible evidence.)

Scientists **will** find a cure for cancer one day.

The movie **is about to** start.

A Read and circle the correct words.

1. Peter thinks that people (will / are going to) live on the moon one day.

2. Look at the dark clouds. It (will / is going to) rain.

3. The door is closed. Olivia has her hand on the doorknob. She is (about to / going to) open the door.

4. These shoes are very comfortable. I (will / am about to) buy them.

Learn & Practice 2

Future Conditional Sentences

- We use future conditional sentences to talk about events or situations that can possibly happen in the present or future.
- We use an *if*-clause to express a possible situation. A main clause shows a result of the *if*-clause.
- We do not use *will* or *be going to* in a conditional clause even though we are talking about the future. We use a simple present in the *if*-clause and a future tense in the main clause.
- When the *if*-clause comes before the main clauses, they are separated with a comma (,). When the main clause comes before the *if*-clause, then they are not separated with a comma (,).

If it **doesn't rain** tomorrow, we**'ll go** on a picnic.

You**'re going to** pass the test if you **study**.

- We sometimes use the simple present in both clauses to express general truths or habitual activities.

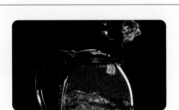

If you **heat** water, it **boils**.

We always **walk** to school if it **doesn't rain**.

A Complete the sentences with the verbs in brackets in the simple present or will.

1. If I ___find___ (find) your book, I will give it to you.

2. She _____ (call) us if she has any problems.

3. If you _____ (go) to the party, I will come with you.

4. If Robert studies hard, he _____ (pass) his exams.

B Complete the sentences, putting the verbs into the correct tense.

1. If people ___travel___ a long distance, they often ___feel___ jet lag. (travel / feel)

2. If air _____, it _____ lighter. (expand / become)

3. If the temperature _____ below 0℃, water _____. (not fall / not freeze)

4. If I _____ to work by car, it _____ thirty-five minutes. (go / take)

Future Time Clauses with *When, Before, and After*

- A future time clause can begin with before, after, and when.
- When a time clause refers to the future, we use the simple present. We don't use *will* or *be going to* in a future time clause.
- We can put the time clause before or after the main clause. They both have the same meaning. Use a comma (,) after the time clause when it comes at the beginning.

Before he **goes** to class tomorrow, he **will eat** breakfast.

When I **get** home this evening, I **will call** you.

- We sometimes use the simple present in both clauses to express general truths or habitual activities.

When babies **are** hungry, they **cry**.

After Katelyn **gets** to work, she always **has** a cup of coffee.

A Use the given verbs to complete the sentences. Give a future meaning to the sentences.

1. Before he ___eats___ breakfast tomorrow, he ___will read___ the newspaper. (eat / read)

2. After we _____ on Tower Bridge, we _____ to Big Ben. (walk / go)

3. When she _____ to London, she _____ a lot. (go / spend)

4. When Sunny _____ us this coming weekend, we _____ her to our favorite family restaurant. (visit / take)

B Match the time clauses with the result clauses.

1. __b__ When our teacher is angry,   a. you get pink.

2. _____ When it gets dark in the desert,   b. she shouts.

3. _____ When you mix red and white,   c. it gets cold.

4. _____ Before I go to class,   d. I usually have a cup of tea.

A Look at Janet's schedule for next week. Then use the future *going to* to make the sentences about her plans.

Monday: Take her new puppy to the veterinarian at 1:00

Tuesday: Take a trip to Disneyland

Wednesday: Exercise at the gym

Thursday: Visit her grandmother

Friday: Go to Ava's farewell party

Saturday: Meet Sandra outside the movie theater at 7:00

Sunday: play badminton with Bob at 10:00

1. She is going to take her new puppy to the veterinarian at 1:00 on Monday.

2. _____

3. _____

4. _____

5. _____

6. _____

7. _____

B Combine the two sentences as in the example.

1.

You put water in the freezer. Then, it turns to ice. (when)

When you put water in the freezer, it turns to ice.

_____

2.

It's usually very hot in the summer. Plants need lots of water. (when)

_____

_____

3.

I sometimes feel really tired. Then, I usually listen to classical music. (if)

_____

_____

4.

Sometimes the temperature reaches -15℃. Then, the lake freezes. (when)

_____

_____

C Read the sentences below. Write sentences using the future will and the prompts in the box.

buy / him / a present	take / the bus / to school
take / an aspirin / and / go to bed	not / sleep

1. I can't ride my bicycle to school because it is snowing. I will take the bus to school.

2. Don't drink coffee before you go to bed.
_____

3. I have a headache and I feel ill.
_____
_____

4. Peter's birthday is on Friday.
_____

D Combine the two sentences as in the example. Give a future meaning to the sentences.

1. I will retire. I will play golf.

→ When I retire, I will play golf. OR I will play golf when I retire. _____

when

2. I don't have money. I will get help from the government.

→ _____

if

3. They will go to Seoul next week. They're going to stay at the Hilton Hotel.

→ _____

when

E What are the following people probably about to do? Make sentences as in the example.

1. The door is closed. Nancy has her hand on the doorknob.

→ She is about to open the door. _____ (open the door)

2. Kyle repaired his car. His hands are dirty. He is holding a bar of soap.

→ _____ (wash his hands)

3. Maggie is putting on her coat and heading for the door.

→ _____ (leave outside)

4. Bill is holding his camera to his eye. He has his finger on the button.

→ _____ (take a picture)

A Look at the example and practice with a partner. Use the words below or invent your own. (Then change roles and practice again.)

1.

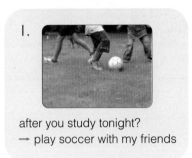

after you study tonight?
→ play soccer with my friends

1.

 What are you going to do after you study tonight?

 After I study tonight, I'll play soccer with my friends.

2.

before you go shopping?
→ go to the gym

3.

after you have dinner?
→ watch a scary movie

4.

after your finish your homework?
→ go to an ice hockey match

B Work with a partner. Ask questions and answer them as in the example.

Lodon /
Big Ben

Rome /
the Colosseum

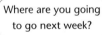

Where are you going to go next week?

I'm going to go to London.

If you go to London, you can see Big Ben. Your turn to ask now!

Paris /
the Eiffel Tower

Egypt /
the Pyramids

New York /
the Empire State Building

Sydney /
the Sydney Opera House

Hawaii /
some palm trees

Seoul /
the Seoul Tower

The Future Tense 31

A **Look and write what the people usually do and what they are doing now.**

1.

| Usually | Now |

go fishing / play baseball

Bobby ___usually goes fishing, but now___

___he is playing baseball___ .

2.
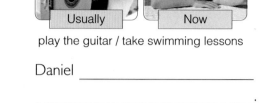

| Usually | Now |

play the guitar / take swimming lessons

Daniel _____

_____ .

3.

| Usually | Now |

listen to classic music / ride a skateboard

Anna _____

_____ .

4.

| Usually | Now |

wash the dishes / watch a movie

They _____

_____ .

B **Are the following sentences present or future? Write *present* or *future* after each one.**

1. Are you going out tonight? → ___future___

2. Where is Jeremy? Is he working? → _____

3. I'm seeing Tiffany on Wednesday. → _____

4. I'm waiting for a call at the moment. → _____

5. We're getting a new car next week. → _____

C **Complete the sentences with the correct form of *used to* and the verb in brackets.**

1.

Michael ___used to jog___ (jog) early in the morning. Now he doesn't jog anymore.

2.

Nancy _____ (not / wear) glasses. Now she wears them.

3.

Tom _____ (watch) TV all the time. Now he almost never watches TV.

D Combine the two sentences in any order, using the time expression in parentheses.

1. The phone rang. I answered the phone. (when)

    → When the phone rang, I answered it.

    → I answered the phone when it rang.

2. I got home. I ate dinner. (after)

    → _____

    → _____

3. I heard the doorbell. I opened the door. (as soon as)

    → _____

    → _____

E Use the given verbs to complete the sentences. Give a future meaning to the sentences.

1. Before I ___go___ (go) to class tomorrow, I ___will eat___ (eat) breakfast.

2. If we _____ (not / have) money, we _____ (get) help from the government.

3. I _____ (read) the textbook before I _____ (take) the final exam next month.

4. When Sarah _____ (visit) us this coming weekend, we _____ (take) her to our favorite family restaurant.

F Look at the notes. Write questions and answers as in the example.

1.
> Concert
> starts 10.
> Leave 7.

Q: What time does the concert start?

A: It starts at 10, so we are leaving at 7.

2.
> Movie
> starts 9.
> Meet Pizza
> Hut 7:30.

Q: _____

A: _____

3.
> Mary
> arrives 8.
> Have dinner
> 8:30.

Q: _____

A: _____

G **Put the verbs in brackets into the simple past or the past progressive.**

1. She ___was watching___ (watch) TV when the telephone ___rang___ (ring).

2. When we _____ (find) the cat, it _____ (play) under the bed.

3. Kevin _____ (have) a shower when the window cleaner _____ (come).

4. Nick and Sally _____ (walk) when it _____ (start) to rain.

H **Fill in the blanks with the words in brackets using _will_ or _be going to_.**

1. A: The phone is ringing and I'm in the shower.
   B: Don't worry Mark, I ___will answer___ (answer) for you.

2. I'm so excited! We _____ (move) to a bigger house next month.

3. My parents _____ (be) very proud. I have passed all the exams.

4. A: There isn't any milk left in the fridge.
   B: Oh, sorry!, I _____ (give) you some juice instead.

5. Look at the clouds. It _____ (rain). You should take an umbrella.

I **Choose the correct answer.**

1. The earth _____ round the sun.
   a. moved   (b.) moves   c. is moving.

2. Sarah _____ a new car last week.
   a. is buying   b. buy   c. bought

3. I _____ when suddenly the dog began to bark.
   a. study   b. studied   c. was studying

4. I _____ home from work when it began to snow.
   a. am walking   b. walk   c. was walking

5. Holly _____ the receiver and dialed the number.
   a. lifts   b. was lifting   c. lifted

6. Rebecca _____ to the gym every day, but now she doesn't.
   a. used to go   b. didn't used to go   c. was going

J Choose the correct question for each answer.

> Do you like movies?   Does he have a new car?
>
> Does Susan walk to school?   Do they love her?

1. _Does he have a new car?_   →   Yes, he does.

2. _____   →   No, they don't.

3. _____   →   Yes, I do.

4. _____   →   Yes, she does.

K Write the correct forms to describe the pictures.

1.

It rains every day.

It _____is raining_____ now.

2.

Kelly plays the guitar every day.

She _____ the guitar now.

3.

They swim in the pool every day.

They _____ in the pool now.

4.

Sean reads a newspaper every day.

He _____ a newspaper now.

L Use the prompts to make sentences in the present progressive tense.

1. I / not ask for / a lot of money.   →   _I'm not asking for a lot of money._

2. She / not listen to / me.   →   _____

3. It / not rain / now.   →   _____

4. She / not wear / a coat.   →   _____

5. We / not enjoy / this film   →   _____

6. You / not eat / much / these days.   →   _____

Quantifying Expressions

• Read and answer the questions.
1. Does Michelle have a lot of apples?
2. Why can't Jessica make an apple pie?
3. How many students are there in your classroom?

Unit Focus

▶ *A Few / Few* vs. *A Little / Little*
▶ *Many, Much, A Lot Of / Lots Of*
▶ *Too Many/Much* vs. *A Lot Of*

A: I have a few apples. I can make an apple pie.
B: If you eat too many apple pies, you'll get fat.

I have very few apples. I can't make an apple pie. I have little money, so I can't buy them.

Learn & Practice 1

A Few / Few vs. A Little / Little

- We use *a few / few* with plural countable nouns to talk about a small number.
- We use *a little / little* with uncountable nouns to talk about small amount.

— *A Few / Few* + Plural Countable Nouns —

a few cookies   **few** cookies

a few people   **few** people

— *A Little / Little* + Uncountable Nouns —

a little water   **little** water

a little bread   **little** bread

- *A few* menas not many, but enough. It has a positive meaning. *Few* and *very few* mean not enough; almost none. It has a negative meaning. We use *very* to emphasize the negative quantity.

- *A little* means not much, but enough. It has a positive meaning. *Little* and *very little* mean not enough; almost none. It has a negative meaning. We use *very* to emphasize the negative quantity.

Alice runs **a few** miles every day.
She drinks a lot of milk and eats **a little** fruit.

In some countries, people have **very little** food, and many people are starving.

A Complete the sentences with *a few*, *few*, *a little* or *little*.

1. It's raining. There are _____few_____ people in the park now.

2. I have _____ friends, so I'm not lonely.

3. There's _____ milk in the fridge. I'm going to the shop to get some.

4. I know _____ Korean. I can understand Korean people.

5. We've got _____ eggs. We can't make an omelet.

6. I'd like to have _____ cheese but many vegetables on my pizza.

Learn & Practice 2

Many, Much, A Lot Of / Lots Of

- We normally use *many* with plural countable nouns in all kinds of sentences (questions, positive/negative sentences).
- We normally use *much* with uncountable nouns in questions and negative sentences. We don't often use *much* in positive sentences.
- We use *a lot of* and *lots of* with both plural countable nouns and uncountable nouns in all kinds of sentences (questions, positive/negative sentences). They are common in an informal style. They mean the same.
- In questions, we use *how much* to ask about the amount of something and *how many* to ask about the number of things.

A: Is there **much** pizza on the table?
B: No, there isn't **much**. There are only two slices.

A : Does Karen have **many** friends?
B: Yes, she has **a lot of (= lots of)** friends.

A: **How many** slices of bread do you eat for breakfast?
   (She wants to know the number.)
B: About five.
A: **How much** coffee do you drink? (She wants to know the amount.)
B: Not much. About three cups.

A Complete the sentences with *many*, *much*, or *a lot of*. In some cases, more than one answer is possible.

1. Do you drink ___much / a lot of___ milk?
2. Sunny doesn't eat _____ meat.
3. How _____ money do you want?
4. How _____ doughnuts does she eat?
5. I like to read. I have _____ books.
6. Is there _____ tea in the cup?

Learn & Practice 3

Too Many/Much vs. A Lot Of
- We use *too many* before plural countable nouns. We use *too much* before singular uncountable nouns.
- A sentence with *too many/much* can have a complaining tone.
- *A lot of* shows a large quantity. No problem is presented. It has a neutral tone.
- *Too many* and *too much* show an excessive quantity. A problem is presented or implied.

A lot of people came to the concert.
We all had a great time.

Too many people came to dinner.
There wasn't enough food for everyone.

There is **too much** noise.

A Fill in the blanks with *a lot of*, *too many*, or *too much*.

1. I can't bear living in big cities because there is ___too much___ noise and pollution.
2. Don't worry, we have _____ food to cook dinner for 10 people.
3. John eats _____ fast food. He should eat more fruit and vegetables.
4. I think I ate _____ pieces of pumpkin pie. Now I feel sick.
5. Jessica is going to bake a cherry pie. She needs _____ cherries.
6. There were _____ people on the bus, so I couldn't get on.
7. I can't eat this soup. It has _____ salt.

A Make questions with *many* or *much* and then answer them with *(a) few* or *(a) little*.

1.

cucumber

Q: Are there many cucumbers?

A: No, there are a few cucumbers.

2.

bread

Q: _____

A: _____

3.

food

Q: _____

A: _____

4.

passenger

Q: _____

A: _____

B Change *a lot of* to *too many* or *too much*. Use *too many* with plural countable nouns. Use *too much* with singular uncountable nouns.

1. There are a lot of cars and trucks in the big city.
→ There are too many cars and trucks in the big city.

2. If I drink a lot of coffee, I won't be able to sleep tonight.
→ _____

3. There is a lot of pollution in the big city.
→ _____

4. There are a lot of children in the park today.
→ _____

5. The teacher gave us a lot of homework.
→ _____

C Complete the sentences. Use *very few* or *very little* + one of these words:

| work | mistakes | countries | gray whales | experience | rain |

1. Your Korean is very good. You make _____*very few mistakes*_____ .

2. That worker has _____. He probably can't do that job.

3. The weather here is very dry in the summer. There is _____.

4. There are _____ in the world. These animals are an endangered species.

5. Some people in my office are very lazy. They do _____.

6. Women are still rare as political leaders. _____ have a woman president.

D Write questions and answer them, as in the example. Use *how many* or *how much*.

1. apples / the fridge → some
   Q: *How many apples are there in the fridge?*____   A: *There are some apples in the fridge.*____

2. bread / the basket → any
   Q: _____   A: _____

3. dresses / your wardrobe → a lot of
   Q: _____   A: _____

4. sugar / the fridge → any
   Q: _____   A: _____

E Make sentences using *there is/are, much/many* or *a little / a few* with the words in the brackets.

1. Today is my birthday. (presents / in my room)
   → *There are many presents in my room.*_____

2. I don't have enough money to buy the storybook. (money / in my pocket)
   → _____

3. My brother, Kevin, is playing with sand on the beach. (sand / on his body)
   → _____

4. It is twelve o'clock midnight. (people / at the bus stop)
   → _____

A Look at the example and practice with a partner. Use the words below or invent your own. (Then change roles and practice again.)

1.

orange juice / ? → a little

1.

How much orange juice would you like?

I'd like a little, please. Thanks.

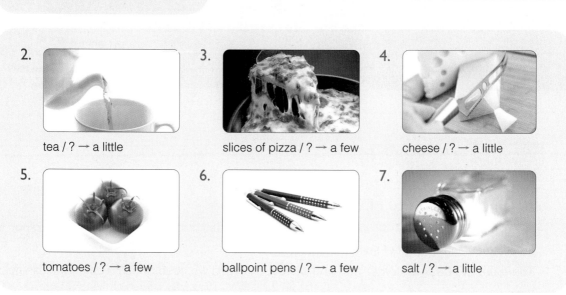

2. tea / ? → a little

3. slices of pizza / ? → a few

4. cheese / ? → a little

5. tomatoes / ? → a few

6. ballpoint pens / ? → a few

7. salt / ? → a little

B Work with a partner. Ask questions with "*Are there any (OR many)...?*" and answer them as in the example.

Are there any supermarkets in your town?

Yes. There are a few (two, a lot of) supermarkets in my town. OR No. There aren't any supermarkets in my town.

Your turn to ask now!

1. supermarkets

2. department stores

3. churches

4. skyscrapers

5. universities

6. foreigners

7. nursing homes

8. fast-food restaurants

9. hospitals

10. factories

11. family restaurants

- Read and answer the questions.
1. How many of the people are standing?
2. Are they all wearing skirts?
3. What are the people doing in the picture?
4. How do they look?

Unit Focus

▶ All, Almost All Of, Most Of, and Some Of
▶ Expressions of Quantity: Subject-Verb Agreement
▶ One Of, None Of

All the people are in the park. All of them are sitting. Almost all of them are wearing jeans. Some of them are wearing T-shirts.

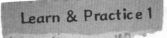

Learn & Practice 1

All, Almost All Of, Most Of, and Some Of

- We use *all, almost all of, most of,* and *some of* to express the quantity of a countable group and to talk about the amount of something uncountable.
- There are two basic patterns –with and without *of.* When we need to use *of,* the noun is specific. If we use *all/most/some* + noun (without of), the noun is general. With *the, all + the* noun and *all of the* + noun are both specific.
- If we use a pronoun or a specific noun (the/this/that/these/my/your... + noun), all/most/some should be followed by *of.*

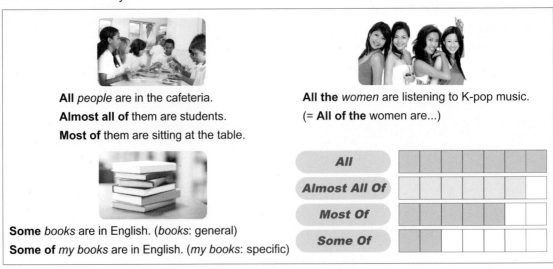

All *people* are in the cafeteria.
Almost all of them are students.
Most of them are sitting at the table.

All the *women* are listening to K-pop music.
(= **All of the** women are...)

Some *books* are in English. (*books*: general)
Some of *my books* are in English. (*my books*: specific)

| All |
| Almost All Of |
| Most Of |
| Some Of |

A: All *Koreans* like kimchi. (*Koreans* is general.)

B: That's not true. My teacher is a Korean and she doesn't like kimchi.

A: Well, all of the *Koreans* that I know like kimchi. (Here, *Koreans* is specific.)

   = All the *Koreans* that I know like kimchi. (Here, *Koreans* is specific.)

A Circle the correct words and check the correct boxes.

	General	Specific
1. (All of / (All)) cars need wheels.	✓	☐
2. (Most / Most of) children like to play.	☐	☐
3. (Some / Some of) these books are very old.	☐	☐
4. (All of / Most) the students in Korea study English.	☐	☐
5. Kevin ate (almost all of / most) his food.	☐	☐
6. (All / All of) cities have the same problems.	☐	☐

Learn & Practice 2

Expressions of Quantity: Subject–Verb Agreement

- When a subject includes an expression of quantity, the verb can be singular or plural. The noun tells you which one to use.

All the **people** in the photo **are** women.
(*People* is plural, so the verb is plural.)

All the **pizza is** here.
(*Pizza* is singular, so the verb is singular.)

All of my **work is** finished.
(*Work* is singular, so the verb is singular.)

Some of my **friends are** playing soccer.
(*Friends* is plural, so the very is plural.)

Some of the **water is** in the glass.
(*Water* is singular, so the verb is singular.)

A Read and choose the correct words.

1. All of that money (is / are) yours.

2. All my friends (lives / live) in Seoul.

3. Most of the flowers (is / are) beautiful.

4. Some of the movie (was / were) interesting.

5. Almost all of the river (is / are) polluted.

6. Most of the countries (has / have) their own language.

Learn & Practice 3

One Of, None Of

- We use *one of* before specific plural nouns (the/those/these/my/your. . . + noun).
- When *one of* + a specific plural noun is the subject of a sentence, the verb that follows must be singular.
- *None of* has a negative meaning and is followed by either a singular or plural verb in the affirmative. In everyday English, both singular and plural verbs are used.

One of my friends **comes** from Korea.
None of the students in this class **come** from Japan.
None of the students in this class **comes** from Japan.

A Look at the pictures and choose the correct words.

1.

One of the players in our soccer team (score / scores) a goal.

2.

(One / None) of the students were late.

3.

One of the women (carries / carry) an umbrella.

4.

One of the passengers (was / were) hurt in the car accident.

5.

(One / None) of these cars are cheap.

6.

(One / None) of the eggs in the basket was broken.

A Look at the pictures. Use the prompts to make sentences using *all* or *none* + *of them*.

1.

be / young men: *All of them are young men.*

women: *None of them is/are women.*

2.

be wearing / skirts: _____

pants: _____

3.

can / swim: _____

fly: _____

4.

be / expensive: _____

cheap: _____

B Look at the picture and complete the sentences with *all the*, *most of the*, *almost all of the*, *some of the* or *none of the*.

1. *All the people* _____ are students.

2. _____ are boys, and some are girls.

3. _____ are wearing ties.

4. _____ are standing.

5. _____ are wearing school uniforms.

6. _____ are sitting at their desks.

7. _____ are raising their hands.

8. _____ are looking at the camera.

C Make sentences using the prompts given.

1. one of / my book / be / in English

→ *One of my books is in English.* _____

2. Most of / the student / in my class / be / smart and witty.

→ _____

3. none of the / student / in my class / understand / the new math topic

→ _____

4. Lotte World / be / one of my favorite / place / in the world

→ _____

D Complete the sentences with a quantity word to make a true statement about specific nouns.

1. *None of the students* _____ in this class come from Japan.

2. *Almost all of the students* _____ in this class speak English.

3. _____ are absent today.

4. _____ in this class want to learn Japanese.

5. _____ in Korea study English in elementary school.

6. _____ have an ID card.

E Correct the mistakes and rewrite the sentences.

1. All of the girls is playing soccer. → *All of the girls are playing soccer.*

2. Almost all of the air in the city are polluted. → _____

3. Some of the girls is wearing skirts. → _____

4. None us can predict the future. → _____

5. One of my favorite movie is *Toy Story*. → _____

6. Almost of all the oceans in the world is polluted.

→ _____

7. Most of my classmates is always on time for class.

→ _____

A Look at the example and practice with a partner. Use the words below or invent your own. (Then change roles and practice again.)

1.

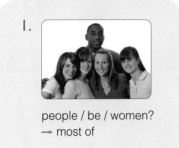

people / be / women?
→ most of

1.

How many of the people are women?

Most of them are women.

2.

women / be wearing hats?
→ all of

3.

students / be wearing jeans?
→ none of

4.

people / be standing?
→ almost all of

B Work with a partner. Look at the table below. Then interview your partner about how the students in class spend their free time.

How many of the students watch TV in their free time?

All the students watch TV in their free time.

Your turn to ask now.

How do the students spend their free time?							
watch TV							all (of)
play sports							almost all of
play computer games							most of
listen to music							some of
like to read books							one of
surf the Net							none of

Unit 7 — *Very, Too,* and *Enough*

• Read and answer the questions.
1. What are Ava and Alice doing now?
2. Why can't Alice wear that blouse?
3. If you have enough money, what will you do with it?

Unit Focus

▶ *Very* and *Too*
▶ *Too* + Adjective (*For* + Noun) + Infinitive
▶ Adjective + *Enough* (+ Infinitive) / *Enough* + Noun

> Ava : That blouse is beautiful, and it's very expensive. Are you going to buy it?
> Alice: Yes, I am. I have enough money to get it. I would like to try this blouse on, but I don't think it is big enough for me.
> Ava: What size is it? If it's 4, it's too small. I think your size is 8.

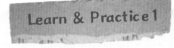

Very and *Too*

- We use *very* and *too* before adjectives. *Very* adds emphasis. It makes the word following it stronger.
- We use *too* to show that something is excessive or more than enough. *Too* shows that there is a problem.

── *Very* + Adjective ──	── *Too* + Adjective ──

This box is **very** heavy, but Tracy can lift it.	This coffee is **too** hot. I can't drink it.

A Complete the sentences with *very* or *too*.

1.

The suitcase is ___very___ heavy, but she can carry it.

2.

The suitcase is _____ heavy. She can't lift it.

Too + Adjective (For + Noun) + Infinitive

- We use *too* + adjective + infinitive. We use *too* in front of an adjective. In the speaker's mind, the use of *too* implies a negative result.
- When we want to determine for whom something is *too* + adjective, we use *for* + noun / object pronoun.

Her feet are too small to wear those shoes.

Those shoes are too big *for Carli* to wear.

Those shoes are too big *for her* to wear.

＊We don't use object pronouns after the full infinitive.   E.g. Those shoes are too big for him to wear them.

Ⓐ **Complete the sentences using *too* and the infinitive.**

1. Hailey is ____*too young to get married*____ . (young / get married)

2. This coffee is _____ . (hot / drink)

3. He was _____ his work. (tired / finish)

4. This smartphone is _____ . (expensive / buy)

5. He is _____ on the phone. (young / talk)

Ⓑ **Complete the sentences using *for* + pronoun and the infinitive.**

1. This hat is too big ____*for him to wear*____ . (he / wear)

2. This soup is too hot _____ . (she / eat)

3. This jacket is too big _____ . (I / wear)

4. This theory is too difficult _____ . (we / understand)

5. The suitcase is too heavy _____ . (I / carry)

6. The magazine is too boring _____ . (they / read)

Adjective + *Enough* (+ Infinitive) / *Enough* + Noun

- We put *enough* after an adjective. *Enough* means sufficiently. In the speaker's mind, the use of *enough* implies a positive meaning. It is followed by to - infinitive.
- *Not + adjective + enough* means that there is a problem. It has a negative meaning. It means not sufficiently.
- We can also use *enough + noun*. *Enough* comes in front of the noun.

Adjective + Enough	Enough + Noun

The shoes are not **big enough**. (= The shoes are too small.)	Some children don't get **enough exercise**.

She is **strong enough to climb** up a tree. (= She can climb up a tree.)	Alice has **enough money to buy** that car.

A Fill in the gaps with *enough* and the word in brackets in the right order.

1. I don't have _____enough sugar_____ (sugar) to make a cake.

2. Last summer it was _____ (hot) to go swimming every day.

3. The room is not _____ (warm).

4. Some people don't get _____ (exercise), so they're overweight.

5. Five hours of sleep isn't _____ (good).

6. Is there _____ (salt) in the soup?

7. Is your English _____ (good) to have a conversation?

8. Do we have _____ (bread) to make sandwiches?

A Look at the pictures and prompts below and write sentences using *too/enough*. Begin with the words given.

1.

be / tired / wash / the dishes

→ Olivia ___is too tired to wash the dishes___ .

2.

be / brave / go / bungee jumping

→ She _____ .

3.

be / hot / for the baby / have a bath

→ The water _____
_____ .

4.

busy / go / to the movie theater / tonight

→ David _____
_____ .

B Look at the pictures. Then answer the questions using the given words.

| heavy | big | sleepy | hot | big |

1. Why can't she lift the TV? → She can't lift it because it is too heavy.

2. Why can't she wear the hat? → _____

3. Why can't he finish his homework? → _____

4. Why can't she eat the pizza? → _____

5. Why can't she wear those shoes? → _____

C Write sentences with the same meaning as the one shown. Use *too* + adjective + *for* + pronoun + infinitive.

1. That house was expensive. We couldn't buy it.
   → *That house was too expensive for us to buy.*

2. The movie was scary. They couldn't watch it.
   → _____

3. The room was cold. She couldn't sit in it.
   → _____

4. The magazine is boring. I can't read it.
   → _____

D Look at the pictures and write sentences using *too/enough* as in the example.

1.

She is strong enough, so she can carry the box.
   → *She is strong enough to carry the box.*

2.

My sister was too sleepy, so she couldn't watch the end of the movie on TV.
   → _____

3.

Do you have enough money? You can buy a T-shirt.
   → _____

4.

We have enough eggs. We can make an omelet.
   → _____

E Complete each statement with an *infinitive* about you.

1. I'm too young _____*to drive a car*_____ .   2. I'm not strong enough _____ .

3. I'm not too old _____ .   4. I don't have enough money _____ .

5. I don't have enough time _____ .   6. I don't speak English well enough _____ .

A Look at the example and practice with a partner. Use the words below or invent your own. (Then change roles and practice again.)

I.

 Can Nora lift that suitcase?

 No, she can't. She can't lift it because it is too heavy. *Or* She can't lift it because it isn't light enough.

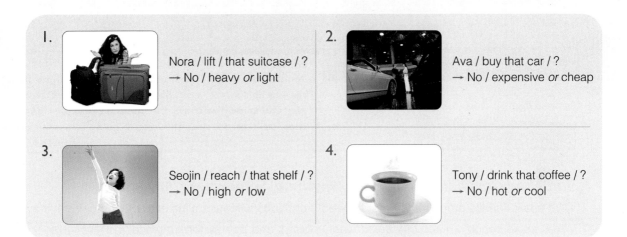

1.
Nora / lift / that suitcase / ?
→ No / heavy *or* light

2.
Ava / buy that car / ?
→ No / expensive *or* cheap

3.
Seojin / reach / that shelf / ?
→ No / high *or* low

4.
Tony / drink that coffee / ?
→ No / hot *or* cool

B Work with a partner. Complete the following sentences. Use a logical infinitive in the completions.

I don't have enough time to go to the party.

Last night I was too tired to finish my homework.

Your turn now!

1. I don't have enough . . .
2. Last night I was too tired . . .
3. I'm not strong enough . . .
4. Yesterday I was too busy . . .
5. I'm too short . . .
6. Yesterday I didn't have enough time . . .

7. A sports car is too expensive . . .
8. I don't have enough money . . .
9. My brother is old enough . . . but too young . . .
10. I know enough English . . . but not enough . . .
11. Yesterday I was really excited enough . . .
12. My sister is old enough . . . but too young . . .

Indefinite Pronouns, *One/Ones*

- Read and answer the questions.
1. Why did Sophie go to the clothing store?
2. Is there anybody with her?
3. Did she find anything nice?

Unit Focus

▶ *Somebody/Anybody, Something/Anything, Somewhere/Anywhere*
▶ *Nobody, Nothing, Nowhere*
▶ *One/Ones*

Sophie is shopping. She is going to a party tonight, but she has nothing to wear. She wants to buy something nice and some new shoes, but she can't find anything that she likes. So, she's thinking of going somewhere else.

Learn & Practice 1

Somebody/Anybody, Something/Anything, Somewhere/Anywhere

- We use indefinite pronouns to refer to people or things without saying exactly who or what they are.
- We use *somebody* (a person), *something* (a thing), and *somewhere* (a place) in affirmative statements.
- We use *anybody, anything,* and *anywhere* for questions and negative statements.

Affirmative	Negative	Question

Lauren is speaking to **somebody** on the phone. She is going **somewhere**.	There isn't **anybody** in the house.	Did you find **anything** to eat?

	Affirmative Statements	Negative Statements	Questions
Unknown people	somebody (= someone)	anybody (= anyone)	anybody (= anyone)
Unknown things	something	anything	anything / *something
Unknown places	somewhere	anywhere	anywhere

I'm thirsty. I want something to drink.
Would you like to have *something to eat?
We saw somebody (= someone) in the dark room.

Do you know anything about this accident?
She lives somewhere near the airport.
Jim didn't talk to anybody (= anyone) after class.

- We use a singular verb after an indefinite pronoun.
  Somebody is in the shop.   Does anyone have a dictionary?

A Choose the correct words.

1. I would like (~~something~~ / anything) to eat.

2. She didn't buy (anything / something) at the store.

3. There is (somebody / anybody) in the room. Who is it?

4. Allison is (somewhere / anywhere) in the countryside.

5. I lost my book yesterday. I left it (somewhere / anywhere).

6. I don't have (something / anything) to wear to the party tomorrow.

Learn & Practice 2

Nobody, Nothing, Nowhere

- We can use *nobody* (= *no one*), *nothing,* and *nowhere* in place of *not anybody/anyone, not anything,* and *not anywhere.*
- When we use *nobody, nothing,* and *nowhere,* we don't use a negative verb (E.g. *isn't, didn't,* etc.).

I know **nothing** about Korean culture.
= I **don't** know **anything** about Korean culture.

We can see **nobody** in the garden.
= We **can't** see **anybody** in the garden.

＊We must use a **singular verb** after an indefinite pronoun. E.g. Nothing **is** in this mailbox.

	Affirmative Statements	Negative Statements	Questions
Unknown people Unknown things Unknown places	nobody (= no one) nothing nowhere		nobody (= no one) nothing nowhere

---

A Write *nobody, nothing* or *nowhere.*

1. We didn't see anybody. → We saw ___nobody / no one___.

2. I didn't say anything. → I said _____.

3. She didn't tell anybody about her plans. → She told _____ about her plans.

4. We aren't going anywhere this summer. → We're going _____ this summer.

5. I won't tell anything. → I will tell _____.

One/Ones

- We use *one* for a singular noun and *ones* for a plural noun. We use the pronoun *one* and *ones* to avoid repeat the noun.
- We can't use *one* or *ones* with an uncountable noun (E.g. *water*)
- *One/ones* and *some/any* are indefinite (like the article *a*). *It* and *they/them* refer to something definite (like the article *the*).

Q: Do you like the white dress?
A: No, I like this **one**.

I don't like the black shoes, but I like the brown **ones**.

This is Japanese food. **It** is good.

Where are my glasses? Do you see **them**?

Ⓐ Complete the sentences with *one* or *ones*.

1. A: Which is your bag? B: The red ___one___ .

2. A: Can I borrow your pencil? B: Sorry, I haven't got _____ .

3. A: Which ruler did you use? B: The _____ on your desk.

4. A: Which jeans fit you better? B: The black _____ .

5. A: Can you lend me a dictionary? B: I'm sorry, I don't have _____ .

6. Which is your car, the red _____ or the blue _____ ?

7. A: Which books are yours? B: The _____ on the table.

A Complete the dialog with *somebody, anybody, somewhere,* or *anywhere.*

1.

A: I can't find my smartphone. I left it _somewhere_ .

B: Did you look in your room?

2.

A: Can you see a woman in the garden?

B: No, I can't see _____ there. What about you, Susan?
   Can you see _____ there?

A: Yes, I can see _____, but I don't know who she is.

3.

A: Are you going on holiday?

B: No, I'm not going _____ because it is raining everywhere.
   What about you? Are you going _____?

A: Yes, I'm going _____ in the country.

4.

A: Do you have friends in Korea?

B: No, I don't know _____ there.

B Rewrite the sentences in brackets so that the noun is not repeated. Use *one* or *ones.*

1. I don't like the red roses, but _____ I like the white ones. _____ (I like the white roses.)

2. I watched all these DVDs. _____ (I must get some new DVDs.)

3. A: Would you like to have a sandwich?
   B: No, thanks. _____ (I already had a sandwich.)

4. This map isn't very good. _____ (The map in the car is better.)

5. A: Which phone did you use?
   B: _____ (The phone on your desk.)

6. This cup is dirty. _____ (Can I have a clean cup?)

Indefinite Pronouns, *One/Ones* **57**

C Complete the sentences with *something*, *anything*, *somebody*, or *anybody*.

1. I have ___something___ in my schoolbag.

2. _____ told me that there was a party at Martin's house.

3. Do you know _____ about animals in Alaska?

4. She has _____ important to say to you.

5. There isn't _____ wrong with Jonathan's eyes.

6. I talked to _____ at the phone company about my bill.

7. We haven't spoken to _____ about it.

D Write the sentences again with *nobody* or *nothing*.

1. There isn't anything in the box. → There's nothing in the box. _____

2. There isn't anybody in the classroom. → _____

3. I don't have anything to do. → _____

4. She didn't buy anything yesterday. → _____

5. He didn't tell anyone about his plans. → _____

6. There wasn't anyone at home. → _____

E Write the sentences again with *anybody* or *anything*.

1. There's nothing in the box. → There isn't anything in the box. _____

2. William plays with nobody at school. → _____

3. There is nothing in the desk drawer. → _____

4. I eat nothing at night. → _____

5. We have nothing for dinner. → _____

6. There was nobody on the bus. → _____

A Look at the example and practice with a partner. Use the words below or invent your own. (Then change roles and practice again.)

I.

 Can you see a woman behind the door?

 No, I can't see anybody there. Can you see anybody there?

 Yes, I can see somebody, but I don't know who she is.

I.
a woman / behind the door / ?
anybody → somebody

2.
a student / in the library?
anybody → somebody

3.
a woman / at the shop?
anybody → somebody

4.
a man / in the movie theater?
anybody → somebody

B Work with a partner. Ask questions and answer them as in the example.

purple dress

black dress

blue skirt

orange skirt

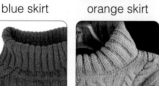
red sweater

green sweater

red T-shirt

green T-shirt

grey socks

pink socks

red sunglasses

yellow sunglasses

pink flip-flops

purple flip-flops

Can I borrow your dress?

Which one do you want?

The black one.

Your turn to ask now!

Indefinite Pronouns, *One/Ones* 59

A Complete the sentences with *many* or *much*.

1. How ___many___ books did you read last year?

2. How _____ money did you spend yesterday?

3. There are _____ cars in the big city.

4. How _____ water do you drink a day?

B Complete the sentences with *a few*, *few*, *a little*, or *little*.

1. I have ___a few___ eggs. I can make an omelet.

2. I know _____ Japanese. I can understand Japanese people.

3. I've got _____ strawberries. I can make some jam.

4. There's _____ milk in the fridge. I'm going to the store.

5. Steve is new in town and has _____ friends here.

C Rewrite the sentences as in the example.

1. Sasha is too young to get dressed herself. (enough / old)
   → Sasha isn't old enough to get dressed herself. _____

2. Joy is too tired to go to the party. (enough / energetic)
   → _____

3. Brandon is too poor to buy the house. (enough / rich)
   → _____

D Complete the sentences with *one* or *ones*.

1. Lisa has lost the 9:00 train. She will take the next ___one___.

2. She hasn't taken a big suitcase. She's carrying a small _____.

3. This T-shirt is too small for me. Can you give me a bigger _____.

4. Which shoes are yours? The _____ under the table are mine.

5. I don't like the white shoes, but I like the brown _____.

E Choose the correct words.

1. All of the money (**is** / are) yours.

2. All of the doors (is / **are**) open.

3. Some of my friends (is / **are**) playing baseball.

4. All of the students in Korea (studies / **study**) English.

5. Almost all of the air in the city (**is** / are) polluted.

F Make sentences using the prompts given.

1. coffee / be / one of / foreign import

   → *Coffee is one of foreign imports.*

2. one of the / student / in my class / always come / late

   → _____

3. none of the / student / in this class / come / from Korea

   → _____

G Choose the right answer.

1. There is _____ waiting for you.

   a. something   b. anybody   c. anything   **d. somebody**

2. I don't want to do _____ today.

   a. something   b. anything   c. anybody   d. somebody

3. A: Are you going on holiday?

   B: No, I'm not going _____ because it is raining everywhere.

   a. nowhere   b. anywhere   c. nobody   d. anybody

H Look at the pictures and complete the sentences with *too* or *very*.

1.

He is _**too**_ lazy.
He doesn't do anything useful.

2.

The weather is _____ nice.
We're going to swim.

3.

Greg was _____ late.
He couldn't catch the plane.

Unit 9 The Passive

- Read and answer the questions.
1. Have you ever been to the Seoul Tower? When?
2. Was the Seoul Tower built in 1896?
3. Are there many famous landmarks in Korea?

Unit Focus
▶ Passive: Affirmative
▶ Passive: Negative
▶ Passive: Questions

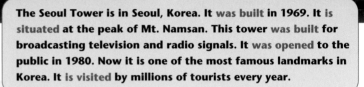

The Seoul Tower is in Seoul, Korea. It **was built** in 1969. It **is situated** at the peak of Mt. Namsan. This tower **was built for** broadcasting television and radio signals. It **was opened** to the public in 1980. Now it is one of the most famous landmarks in Korea. It **is visited** by millions of tourists every year.

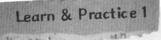
Learn & Practice 1

Passive: Affirmative (*Be* + V-*ed*)

- We use the passive when we focus on what happened rather than who did it. The actor (subject) of the verb comes after *by*. The object of the active voice sentence becomes the subject of the passive voice sentence.

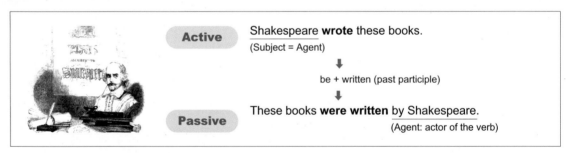

| Active | Shakespeare **wrote** these books. |
| | (Subject = Agent) |

⬇

be + written (past participle)

⬇

| Passive | These books **were written** by Shakespeare. |
| | (Agent: actor of the verb) |

- We use the passive when we don't know who did something, or who does something is obvious or not important. We don't use the agent (*by* + actor).

Hamlet was written by Shakespeare.   My smartphone was stolen.
(The person who wrote it is important to   (We don't know who stole it, but the important fact is
the writer's meaning.)   that it was stolen.)

	Subject	Be	Verb + -*ed*	By	Object (Agent)
Present/ Past Passive	I	am/was			them/ her/ Tom.
	He/She/It/Thing	is/was	loved	by	
	You/We/They/Things	are/were			

- We form the passive with the verb *be* and the past participle (verb + -ed) of the main verb.

A Choose the correct words.

1. The picture (painted / (was painted)) by Derek.

2. The temple (was destroyed / were destroyed).

3. My mom (loves / is loved) me.

4. The teacher (helps / is helped) us.

5. Your life (is changed / changed) by books.

6. The work (was done / did) by him.

B Change the verbs to the passive form.

1. Shakespeare wrote Othello. → Othello ___*was written*___ by Shakespeare.

2. Tom invited me to the party. → I _____ to the party by Tom.

3. They bake the bread. → The bread _____ by them.

4. The teacher teaches us. → We _____ by the teacher.

5. People speak English in Toronto. → English _____ in Toronto.

Learn & Practice 2

Passive: Negative (*Be + Not + V-ed*)
- We use *not* after the verb *be* to make negative sentences in the passive.

Some food **aren't loved** by children.
→ Children don't love some food.

The window **wasn't broken** by them.
→ They didn't break the window.

Subject	Be	Not	Verb + -ed	
I	am/was			The room **wasn't cleaned** by her.
He/She/It/Thing	is/was	not	invited.	The thief **isn't caught**.
You/We/They/Things	are/were			Bananas **aren't grown** in Korea.

A Write the negative forms.

1. The letter is written by me. → The letter isn't written by me.

2. These toys were made by him. →

3. The song was sung by Lady Gaga. →

4. This machine was invented by John. →

5. This book is read by many students. →

6. My wallet was stolen on the bus. →

Learn & Practice 3

Passive: Questions (*Be* + Subject + V-*ed*...?)

- To make *yes/no* questions, we put the verb *be* before the subject. *Yes/no* questions end with a question mark (?).
- In short answers, we only use *yes* or *no*. We add *not* if the answer is negative.

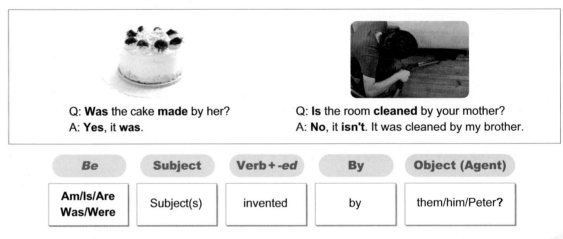

Q: **Was** the cake **made** by her?
A: **Yes**, it **was**.

Q: **Is** the room **cleaned** by your mother?
A: **No**, it **isn't**. It was cleaned by my brother.

Be	Subject	Verb + -ed	By	Object (Agent)
Am/Is/Are Was/Were	Subject(s)	invented	by	them/him/Peter?

A Write questions and answer them.

1. My digital camera was stolen. Q: Was your digital camera stolen? A: Yes, __it was__.

2. The office was cleaned. Q: _____ A: No, _____.

3. The thief was arrested yesterday. Q: _____ A: Yes, _____.

4. English is spoken by many people. Q: _____ A: Yes, _____.

5. Two hundred people were employed.
  Q: _____ A: No, _____.

A Look at the pictures and prompts. Make sentences using the simple present passive, as in the example.

1.

Volkswagen cars / make / Germany

→ <u>Volkswagen cars are made in Germany.</u>

_____

2.

a lot of rice / eat / Korea

→ _____

_____

3.

Coca-Cola / produce / the USA

→ _____

_____

4.

snails / eat / France

→ _____

_____

B Change the sentences from active to passive. Include the *by*-phrase only if necessary.

1. Scott built that house. → <u>That house was built by Scott.</u>

2. Someone stole my camera. → <u>My camera was stolen. (someone: unnecessary)</u>

3. People grow rice in Korea. → _____

4. Do people speak English in Korea? → _____

5. The police solved the mystery. → _____

6. The coach always encourages the trainees. → _____

7. Someone built this house in 1999. → _____

8. Someone destroyed the temple in 1900. → _____

9. Helen usually prepares breakfast. → _____

C Look at the pictures. Read questions and answer them as in the example.

1.

Thomas Edison

Q: Who invented the light bulb?

A: The light bulb was invented by Thomas Edison.

2.

Edwin Binney and Harold Smith

Q: Who invented the crayons?

A: _____

_____

3.

Thomas Sullivan

Q: Who invented the tea bag?

A: _____

_____

4.

J. K. Rowling

Q: Who wrote the *Harry Potter* books?

A: _____

_____

D Change the sentences from active to passive. Use the *by*-phrase when necessary. Some of the sentences are questions.

1. People drink Coca-Cola all over the world.

→ Q: Coca-Cola is drunk all over the world. _____

2. Did John Pemberton invent the drink in 1886?

→ Q: _____ A: Yes, it was.

3. The McDonald brothers opened the first Mcdonald's restaurant.

→ _____

4. Do all children need love and understanding?

→ _____

5. People eat more than 40 million hamburgers every day.

→ _____

6. Do people play soccer in most countries of the world?

→ _____

A Look at the example and practice with a partner. Use the words below or invent your own. (Then change roles and practice again.)

1.

the light bulb / invent /
Shakespeare / ?
→ No / Thomas Edison

1.

 Was the light bulb invented by Shakespeare?

 No it wasn't. It was invented by Thomas Edison.

2.

the Eiffel Tower / design
/ Leo Tolstoy / ?
→ No / Gustave Eiffel

3.

The Mona Lisa / paint /
Michelangelo / ?
→ No / Leonardo da Vinci

4.

the telephone / invent / Walt
Disney / ?
→ No / Alexander Graham Bell

B Work with a partner. Ask questions and answer them as in the example.

1. Dr. John Pemberton / invent /
Coca-Cola / in 1886

2. Louis Lassen / make / the first
hamburger / in 1895

3. Dick and Mac McDonald / open /
a drive-in hamburger restaurant /
in 1948

4. People / do not know / the
ingredients of Coca-Cola

5. People / eat / more than 40 million
hamburgers / every day

Dr. John Pemberton invented
Coca-Cola in 1886.
Can you change this sentence
from active to passive?

Yes, I can.
Coca-Cola was invented in 1886
by Dr. John Pemberton.

Your turn to ask!

• Read and answer the questions.
1. What are the children doing in the picture?
2. We are in a classroom. If an earthquake hits, what should we do?

Unit Focus

▶ Expressing Ability: *Can* and *Could*
▶ Using *Be Able To*
▶ Expressing Advice: *Should, Ought To, Had Better*
▶ Expressing Permission: *Can* and *May*

If you are in a building during an earthquake, you should stay away from windows or anything heavy like a bookcase. You should drop to the ground and take cover under a desk or a table. If the desk moves, you should move with it. Otherwise, you had better remain where you are until the earthquake is over. In any case, you ought to stay calm and encourage others to do the same.

Learn & Practice 1

Expressing Ability: *Can* and *Could*

- We use *can* or *can't (cannot)* to express ability in the present or future, and *could* or *couldn't* + a base verb to express ability in the past.
- *Can* and *could* take the same form for all persons. There is no *-s* ending in the third person singular.
- We form questions by putting *can* or *could* before the subject.

Ability

Anna **could** play badminton last year, but she **can't** play badminton now.

Ten years ago, I **couldn't** swim, but I **can** swim well now.

Ⓐ Complete the sentences with *can, can't, could,* or *couldn't.*

1. Suddenly all the lights went out. We ___couldn't___ see a thing.

2. A cat _____ climb trees, but it _____ fly.

3. _____ you write with your left hand?

4. _____ you speak English when you were younger?

Using *Be Able To*

- We can use *be (am/is/are/was/were) able to* instead of *can* or *could* to talk about ability in the present, the future, and the past.

Now	Past	Future
Jennifer **is able to** play the violin.	She **wasn't able to** finish the test.	I'll **be able to** go to Korea tomorrow.

A Make sentences with the same meaning. Use *be able to.*

1. I couldn't finish my homework last night. → I wasn't able to finish my homework last night.

2. Next year I can ride a bicycle. → _____

3. They can play volleyball. → _____

4. We couldn't go on a picnic. → _____

Expressing Advice: *Should, Ought To, Had Better*

- We use *should* and *ought to* give advice or an opinion. *Should* and *ought to* mean this is a good idea to do something. We usually don't use *ought to* in question, negative sentences, and short answers. We use *should* instead.

- We use *had better* to express a strong recommendation in specific situations, not general ones. If you want to talk about general situations, you must use *should*. *Had better* usually implies a warning about possible bad consequences. It is stronger than *should* or *ought to*.

General	General	Specific
In Korea, you **ought to** bow when you greet someone.	You **shouldn't** watch TV so much.	It's raining. You **had better** take an umbrella.

- *Had better* contains the word *had*, but it refers to the present or the future, not to the past.
- Negative: *had better* + **not** + base verb (E.g. We **had better not** wait.)

A Make sentences with *should* or *shouldn't*.

1. Jessica got a bad cold. → <u>She shouldn't eat ice cream.</u> (eat / ice cream)

2. Tom has broken his leg. → _____ (stay / in bed)

3. Jane isn't doing well at school. → _____ (hang out / with friends)

4. Sarah's clothes don't fit her. → _____ (lose weight)

B Complete the sentences as in the example.

1. You <u>had better not talk</u> (talk, had better, not) loudly in class.

2. Tim _____ (eat, had better, not) the whole cake.

3. We _____ (study hard, ought to) to prepare for the exam.

4. You _____ (your hands, ought to, wash) before dinner.

Learn & Practice 4

Expressing Permission: Can and May

- We use *can* and *may* to indicate that someone is allowed to do something. *May not* and *can't* are used to deny permission. *May* is a more polite expression than *can*.
- We use *may I*, *could I*, and *can I* to ask permission to do something. *May I* is the most polite, or formal, of the three. *Could I* is more polite or formal than *can I*. We use *can I* when we know the other person very well.

You **can** use a dictionary during the test.

You **may** go home now if you want.

Q: **May (Could) I** see your tickets?
A: Yes, of course.

A Read the underlined words and write *ability* or *permission*.

1. You <u>may</u> use the air conditioner if it's hot in here. → <u>permission</u>

2. <u>May</u> I speak to Jennifer please? → _____

3. My father <u>can</u> speak five languages. → _____

4. You <u>can</u> use my phone if you want to. → _____

5. A: <u>Can</u> I park here? B: I'm sorry. I'm afraid you can't. → _____

6. My mother <u>can</u> get up early every morning. → _____

Super Writing

A Complete the following sentences to say what the girl in the picture can do now, what she could do when she was five years old, and what she will be able to do when she is 20.

five years old	now (age 10)	future (age 20)
read a book	ride a bicycle	drive a car
eat with chopsticks	play badminton	get a good job
drink milk	draw pictures	meet a boyfriend
watch TV	go to a movie	ride a snowboard

1. When she was five years old, _____ *she could read a book* _____.

2. Now, _____ *she can ride a bicycle* _____.

3. When she is 20, _____ *she will be able to drive a car* _____.

4. When she was five years old, _____.

5. Now, _____.

6. When she is 20, _____.

7. When she was five years old, _____.

8. Now, _____.

9. When she is 20, _____.

10. When she was five years old, _____.

11. Now, _____.

12. When she is 20, _____.

B Look at the pictures and make sentences using *you can/can't* with words or expressions from the box.

1.

You can park here.

2.

_____

3.

_____

have coffee
cross the road
park
mobile phones
ride a bicycle
smoke

4.

_____

5.

_____

6.

_____

C Read the situations and make sentences with *had better* or *bad better not* as in the example.

1. Abby feels very tired. (get some rest / work so hard)

   → *She had better get some rest.* → *She had better not work so hard.*

2. Justin wants to lose weight. (jog every morning / eat fast food too much)

   → _____ → _____

3. Nicole can never wake up early in the morning so she's always late for school.
   (use an alarm clock / go to bed late at night)

   → _____ → _____

D You are telling your younger brother what he should or shouldn't do.

1.

   He doesn't wash his hands.

   → *You should wash your hands.* _____

2.

   He doesn't eat breakfast every morning.

   → _____

3.

   He goes to bed late every night.

   → _____

E Make sentences with the same meaning. Use *be able to* or *ought to*.

1. It's winter now. My friends and I can go skiing.

   → *It's winter now. My friends and I are able to go skiing.* _____

2. Dan has a terrible headache. He should take an aspirin.

   → _____

3. I can't go ice skating now, but I could go ice skating last winter.

   → _____

4. You should brush your teeth after every meal.

   → _____

5. We can't go mountain climbing now, but we can go mountain climbing tomorrow.

   → _____

A Look at the example and practice with a partner. Use the words below or invent your own. (Then change roles and practice again.)

1.

 Can you play soccer?

 Yes, I can.

 OK. Let's play soccer in the morning.

1. 	2. 	3. 
play soccer? / Yes → OK / in the morning	make spaghetti? / Yes → OK / in the afternoon	ride a horse? / Yes → OK / in the afternoon
4. 	5. 	6. 
go to the beach? / Yes → OK / in the morning	make sandwiches? / Yes → OK / in the afternoon	play table tennis? / Yes → OK / in the morning

B Work with a partner. Give advice in these situations.

You should go home and get some rest.

I have a bad cold and I'm in my classroom. What should I do?

Your turn now!

1. Your partner: I have a bad cold and I'm in my classroom. What should I do?

2. Your partner: I often go to bed late and get up late. What should I do?

3. Your partner: I ask for money from my parents every day. What should I do?

4. Your partner: When it's cold outside, I only wear a T-shirt. What should I do?

5. Your partner: Someone stole my bicycle. What should I do?

6. Your partner: My girlfriend/boyfriend broke up with me and I'm really sad! What should I do?

- Read and answer the questions.
1. Does the boy have to go to the doctor?
2. What do you have to do today/tomorrow?
3. What did you have to do yesterday? Why?

Unit *Focus*

▶ *Must, Have To,* and *Have Got To* to Express Obligation and Necessity
▶ *Not Have To* and *Must Not* to Express Lack Of Necessity and Prohibition
▶ *May, Might,* and *Could* to Express Possibility
▶ Making Logical Conclusions: *Must*

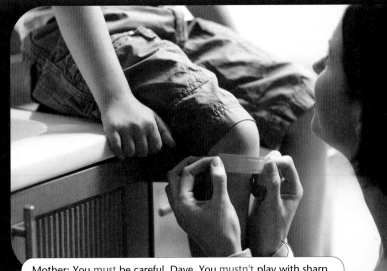

Mother: You must be careful, Dave. You mustn't play with sharp knives.
Dave: Do we have to go to the doctor, mom?
Mother: No, we don't have to go to the doctor. You'll be all right.

Learn & Practice 1

Must, Have To, and *Have Got To* to Express Obligation and Necessity

- We use *Must* and *have to* to express obligation or necessity.
- *Must* is more stronger than *have to*. We use *must* for rules, signs, or strong advice. When we use *must*, we have no choice.
- There is no past form of *must* or *have got to*. We use *have to* to form all the other tenses.
- *Have got to* has the same meaning as *have to*, but we use it mostly in informal spoken English. We use it in affirmative statements. We don't often use it in negative statements or questions.

You **must** do your homework.

Did you **have to** wait for him?

Kathy **has (got) to** practice the violin now.

	Statements	Questions
Present or Future	I **must** study for the test now/tomorrow. They **have (got) to** study for the test now/tomorrow.	Q: **Does** she **have to** work? A: **Yes**, she **does**. / **No**, she **doesn't**. Do I **have to** work? A: **Yes**, you do. / **No**, you **don't**.
Past	We **had to** study for the test last night.	Q: **Did** they **have to** study for the test last night? A: **Yes**, they **did**. / **No**, they **didn't**.

＊We use *must* for questions less often.

A Complete the sentences with the words in brackets.

1. You _____ *must eat* _____ (eat / must) more fruit and vegetables.

2. I _____ (hard / study / have to) for the test.

3. _____ (wear / have to / I) a helmet?

4. They _____ (leave / have got to) now.

5. We _____ (study / had to) last night.

6. _____ (have to / you / buy) some toothpaste yesterday?

Learn & Practice 2

Not Have To and Must Not to Express Lack of Necessity and Prohibition

- *Have to* and *must* have similar meanings in the affirmative, but in the negative, they have very different meanings. We use *must not (= mustn't)* to tell someone not to do something. It means that something is against the law or rules or it isn't right. There is no choice.
- We use *not have to* to show that something is not necessary. There is another possibility or a choice.

You **mustn't** use your cellphones. (It's against the rule. There is no choice.)

Tomorrow is Saturday. We **don't have to** go to school. (It's not necessary.)

I **didn't have to** get up early on weekends. (It was not necessary.)

A Complete the sentences with the correct helping verbs.

1. You __mustn't__ go near the kangaroo. It's dangerous.

2. You _____ drive over 50 miles an hour.

3. She _____ clean her room.
   Her mother is going to clean her room for her.

4. Mike is very fat. He _____ eat much chocolate and candies.
   He _____ drink a lot of water and fruit juice.

> mustn't (x 3)
>
> must
>
> doesn't have to

May, Might, and *Could* to Express Possibility

- We use *may*, *might*, or *could* to express possibility in the present or future. *May, might,* and *could* mean "perhaps."
- We use *may not* and *might not* in negative sentences, but not *could not*. We use these structures to express that something will possibly not happen. We don't contract *may* and *might* with *not* when they express possibility.

That's dangerous! She **may/might/could** fall!   Mary **may/might not** know how to find our house.

A Read the underlined words and write *possibility, ability,* or *permission.*

1. Jack might know the answer.   →   possibility

2. She could lift the box.   →   _____

3. You may come into the room.   →   _____

4. It might not rain tomorrow.   →   _____

Making Logical Conclusions: *Must*

- We use *must* and *can't* to draw definite conclusions about present situations based on what we know. When we are almost 100 percent sure that something is true, we use *can't*.

Pete: I'm looking for Jennifer. Where is she?
Ashley: She **must** be in the library. (95% certainty)
Evan: She **may/might/could** be in the classroom.(less than 50% certainty)
Diane: I saw her in the cafeteria a minute ago, she **can't** be in the library.
          (almost 100% sure)

A Complete the sentences with *must,* or *can't of* the verbs in brackets.

1. They _____must be_____ (be) twins. They are absolutely identical.

2. We had lunch half an hour ago. You _____ (be) hungry.

3. Jessica is coughing and sneezing. She _____ (have) a cold.

A Look at the pictures and make sentences with *must* or *mustn't*.

1.

you / bring / dogs / here

→ You mustn't bring dogs here.

2.

you / be quiet / in class

→ _____

3.

you / tell a lie / to your teacher

→ _____

4.

you / do exercise / for your health

→ _____

B Look at the following instructions. Then write sentences with *mustn't* or *don't have to*.

1. It's isn't necessary for you to wear a suit to the office.
   → You don't have to wear a suit to the office.

2. It is forbidden to smoke on the train.
   → You mustn't smoke on the train.

3. It is forbidden to touch pictures in the museum.
   → _____

4. It isn't necessary for you to go to school today.
   → _____

5. It isn't necessary for you to stay in your seat throughout the flight.
   → _____

6. It is forbidden to spend your time playing video games.
   → _____

7. It isn't necessary for you to finish your homework by tomorrow.
   → _____

Helping Verbs 2 **77**

C Look at the pictures and prompts and write questions and answers. Use *have (got) to.*

1.

Jake / go to the drugstore?
→ Yes / buy some medicine

Q: Does Jake have to go to the drugstore?

A: Yes, he does. He has (got) to buy some

medicine.

2.

Susan / go to the grocery store?
→ Yes / get some vegetables

Q: _____

A: _____

3.

Ava / go shopping?
→ Yes / get a new dress

Q: _____

A: _____

_____

4.

Josh / stay home tonight?
→ Yes / study Korean

Q: _____

A: _____

_____

D You are talking about your neighbors. Complete the sentences using *must* or *can't.*

1. There are no lights on.   →   _____They must be out_____ . (be out)

2. They've bought a new car.   →   _____ . (make a lot of money)

3. We never see any children.   →   _____ . (have any children)

4. They always buy a lot of fresh food. → _____ . (like to eat well)

E Talk about possible happenings. Make sentences as in the example.

1. Do you think it will snow this afternoon? (may)

   → It may snow this afternoon. _____

2. Do you think they'll be waiting for us? (may not)

   → _____

3. Do you think she will be caught in traffic. (could)

   → _____

4. Do you think Amy will be able to find out our house? (might not)

   → _____

A Look at the example and practice with a partner. Use the words below or invent your own. (Then change roles and practice again.)

1.

 I can't find Lisa anywhere. I wonder where she is.

 She could be in the park. She may be jogging.

1.
Lisa?
→ in the park / jog

2.
Emily?
in the library /
study history

3.
Kate and Eric?
in the room /
do their homework now

4.
Toni?
in her room /
talk to her friend

B You and your partner want to go camping. Look at the pictures and say what you must / mustn't / don't have to.

1.
take / medicine

2.
prepare / enough food

Do I have to take medicine with me?

When you go camping, you must take medicine with you.

Your turn to ask!

3.
take / a tent

4.
bring / a flashlight

5.
ask for money from
my parents

6.
bring / campfire wood

4.
think / in advance about
the possible dangers

Helping Verbs 2 79

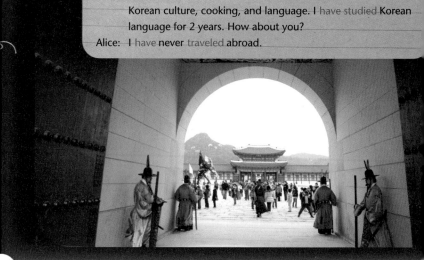

- Read and answer the questions.
1. Have you ever traveled abroad?
2. Have you been to Korea before? If yes, when?
3. Are you interested in Korean culture?

Alice: Have you ever traveled abroad?
Kevin: Yes, I have. I have been to Korea three times. I'm interested in Korean culture, cooking, and language. I have studied Korean language for 2 years. How about you?
Alice: I have never traveled abroad.

Unit Focus

▶ Present Perfect: Meaning
▶ Present Perfect: Forms
▶ Present Perfect: Negative Statements and Questions

Learn & Practice 1

Present Perfect: Meaning

- We use the form of *have/has* + past participle for the present perfect.
- We use the present perfect for an action or situation that happened at some unspecified time in the past. The exact time is not mentioned because it is not important. We put more emphasis on the action.

Hyein **has bought** a new smartphone.
(When did she buy it? We don't mention the exact time because it isn't important. What is important is the fact that she's got a new smartphone.)

- We use the present perfect for an action that started in the past and is still continuing in the present.

Isabella **has been** a math teacher since 2009.
She **has studied** math for 20 years.
(She started working as a math teacher in 2009 and she still is a teacher.)

- We use the present perfect for an action that has recently finished and its result is visible in the present.

They **have finished** their shopping.
(We can see that they have finished their shopping because they're leaving the supermarket and there are bags in their shopping cart.)

A Write *has* or *have*.

1. Jamie ___has___ never read a novel.

2. Nick and Molly _____ arrived in New York.

3. They _____ already finished their shopping.

4. I _____ washed the car.

5. Kelly _____ traveled abroad.

6. Peter _____ painted the wall.

Learn & Practice 2

Present Perfect: Forms

Present	Past	Past Participle	Present	Past	Past Participle
be	was/were	been	break	broke	broken
eat	ate	eaten	do	did	done
know	knew	known	see	saw	seen
meet	met	met	tell	told	told
read	read	read	go	went	gone
have	had	had	fall	fell	fallen
teach	taught	taught	write	wrote	written
lose	lost	lost	give	gave	given
cut	cut	cut	take	took	taken
catch	caught	caught	study	studied	studied
work	worked	worked	live	lived	lived

A Complete the sentences with the present perfect of the verbs in brackets.

1. He ___has worked___ (work) in France.　　2. They _____ (be) to Mexico City.

3. She _____ (finish) breakfast.　　4. It _____ (rain) for three days.

5. We _____ (eat) lunch.　　6. My dad _____ (give up) smoking.

B Make sentences as in the example.

1. The teacher / arrive　　　　→ *The teacher has arrived.*

2. The students / leave　　　　→ _____

3. The exams / finish　　　　　→ _____

4. Steve / break / his leg　　　→ _____

5. She / see / this movie / before　→ _____

Present Perfect: Negative Statements and Questions

- To make a negative sentence, we put *not* between *have/has* and the past participle.
- *Have/has* is placed before the subject to make a *yes/no* question in the present perfect.

We **haven't** eaten Korean food before.
We want to try it.

Q: **Have** you **worked** here long**?**
A: **No**, I **haven't.**

Negative

I/You We/They	have not (= haven't)	
He/She/It	has not (= hasn't)	lived here.

Questions

Have	I/you/ we/they	
Has	he/she/it	**made** a kite?

Q: **Have** you **finished** your homework? A: **Yes**, I **have.**
Q: **Has** she **found** a new job? A: **No**, she **hasn't.**
Q: **Have** they **been** in Canada since 2008? A: **Yes**, they **have.**

Ⓐ Complete the negative sentences with the words on the left.

1. (not / arrive) → They ____haven't arrived____ at the airport.

2. (not / play) → She _____ the piano since last year.

3. (not / ride) → I _____ a horse before.

4. (not / work) → They _____ for a bank.

Ⓑ Make *yes/no* questions and complete the answers.

1. Alex has passed his driving test. Q: _Has Alex passed his driving test?_ A: Yes, ___he has___ .

2. She has seen a ghost. Q: _____ A: No, _____.

3. Laura has lost weight. Q: _____ A: Yes, _____.

4. They have been here for a long time. Q: _____ A: No, _____.

A Choose and make the sentences in the present perfect tense.

live on the farm all his life	eat at that restaurant many times
ride a horse before	be a teacher since 2010

1.

Steve ___has lived on the farm all his life___.

2.

Erika _____.

3.

They _____.

4.

Kathy _____.

B Look at the pictures and write questions and answers. Use the present perfect tense.

1.

Ava / buy / a new / camera / ?
→ No / smartphone

Q: _Has Ava bought a new camera?_

A: _No, she hasn't. She has bought a new_

smartphone.

2.

Ryan and Mary / travel / by helicopter / ?
→ No / train

Q: _____

A: _____

_____

3.

Peter / live / in France / ?
→ No / in Korea

Q: _____

A: _____

_____

4.

Lisa / lose / her phone / ?
→ No / passport

Q: _____

A: _____

_____

Present Perfect 1 83

C Read and make questions and answer them as in the example.

	go to Europe	try bungee jumping	see a scary movie before
Elizabeth	Yes	Yes	No
Rachel and Ben	No	No	Yes

1. Q: Has Elizabeth gone to Europe?   A: Yes, she has.

2. Q: _____ A: _____

3. Q: _____ A: _____

4. Q: _____ A: _____

5. Q: _____ A: _____

6. Q: _____ A: _____

D Look at the box and make sentences. What has Andy done and what hasn't he done?

The Things He Has Done	The Things He Hasn't Done
1. ride a donkey	2. ride an ostrich
3. read 'War and Peace'	4. read 'The Lord of the Rings'
5. break a leg	6. listen to K-pop music
7. take Taekwondo lessons	8. travel all over the world

1. William has ridden a donkey.   2. _____

3. _____ 4. _____

5. _____ 6. _____

7. _____ 8. _____

A Look at the example and practice with a partner. Use the words below or invent your own. (Then change roles and practice again.)

1.

Have you seen the Statue of Liberty?

No, I haven't. I haven't seen the Statue of Liberty.

1.

you / see / the Statue of Liberty / ?
→ No

2.

Mia / eat good food / ?
→ No

3.

they / buy / tickets / to a Broadway show / ?
→ No

4.

they / arrive in Seoul / ?
→ No

5.

they / enjoy Seoul / ?
→ No

6.

you / see / Namdaemun / ?
→ No

B Work with a partner. Imagine that you and your partner are going camping for the weekend. Look at the list below. What have you done? What have you not done? Take turns to ask and answer questions as in the example.

- find the tend (O)
- buy a sleeping bag (X)
- find the campground (O)
- buy bottles of water (O)
- find a digital camera (X)
- take a camping lantern (O)
- find camping equipment (X)
- watch the weather forecast (O)

Have you found the tent?
Yes, I have.

A **Make sentences in the passive form.**

1. Antoni Gaudi	build the church
2. Wright Brothers	invent airplanes
3. Gustave Eiffel	design and build the Eiffel Tower
4. O. Henry	write *The Last Leaf*
5. Ernest Hemingway	write *The Old Man and the Sea*
6. Leonardo da Vinci	draw *the Mona Lisa*

1. The church was built by Antoni Gaudi.

2. _____

3. _____

4. _____

5. _____

6. _____

B **Look at the pictures and write questions and answers. Use the present perfect tense.**

1.

he / buy / an MP3 player / ?
No → a new smartphone

Q: Has he bought an MP3 player?

A: No, he hasn't. He has bought a new smartphone.

2.

Tiffany / travel / by airplane / ?
No → by train

Q: _____

A: _____

C **Read the situations. Make questions with *May I . . .?* or *Can I . . .?* as in the example.**

1.

You ask your mother for permission to watch TV with your sister.

→ Can I watch TV with my sister?

2. It's quite hot in the room, and you want to open the window. What do you say to your father?

→ _____

3. You want to use the phone in your teacher's office. What do you say to her?

→ _____

D **Read the Hotel Rules and complete the sentences as in the example.**

Hotel Rules

1. Do not smoke in your room.
2. Do not take food into your room.
3. Pay for your room on the day you arrive.
4. Return to the hotel by 10:00 p.m. every night.
5. Leave your key at the reception desk when you go out.
6. Leave your room at 9:00 a.m. on the day you leave.

1. You mustn't smoke _____ in you room.

2. _____ into your room.

3. _____ on the day you arrive.

4. _____ by 10:00 p.m. every night.

5. _____ at the reception desk when you go out.

6. _____ at 9:00 a.m. on the day you leave.

E **Look at the prompts given. Ask and answer questions, as in the example.**

1. she / go to the supermarket / yesterday → do some shopping

   Q: Why did she go to the supermarket yesterday?

   A: Because she had to do some shopping.

2. he / go to the post office / yesterday → post some letters

   Q: _____

   A: _____

F **Make sentences using *had better* (✓) or *had better not* (X) and the words in brackets.**

1. A: I'm going to an expensive restaurant tonight. (X / wear / jeans)

   B: You'd better not wear jeans.

2. A: Bill is going on a trip, but the weather is cold. (✓ / take / a jacket)

   B: _____

3. A: I missed the bus and I don't want to be late for work. (✓ / take / a taxi)

   B: _____

4. A: Olivia is leaving for the airport in five minutes. (X / forget / her passport)

   B: _____

• Read and answer the questions.

1. How long have they been on holiday?
2. Have they swum in the river?
3. Have you ever eaten dinner yet?
4. Have you ever met a Hollywood star? Who?

Unit *Focus*

▶ Present Perfect: *For* and *Since*
▶ Present Perfect: *Ever* and *Never*
▶ *Have Gone (To)* vs. *Have Been (To)*
▶ Present Perfect: *Already, Yet,* and *Just*

Ava married Steve last April. She has been married since April. Ava and Steve have been on holiday for a week. They've visited a lot of tropical beaches and they've swum in the blue sea. Have they eaten breakfast yet? Yes, they have already eaten breakfast.

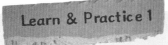

Present Perfect: *For* and *Since*

- We use the present perfect to talk about an action or situation that started in the past and continues up to the present. We often use the present perfect with *for* and *since*.
- We use *for* and *since* with the present perfect to talk about how long the action or situation has continued up to the present.
- We use *for* when we are talking about a length of time. We use *since* when we are talking about the start of the period.

They are on vacation in Seoul.
They arrived in Seoul on Monday.
Today is Saturday.
Q: *How long* **have** they **been** in Seoul?
A: They **have been** in Seoul **since** Monday.
They **have been** in Seoul **for** five days.

	For		**Since**
for	three days four months five weeks two days three hours twenty minutes a minute a long time	since	2011 last year (last) October (last) Thursday yesterday this morning 9:00 this morning

 Complete the sentences with *for* or *since*.

1. He has worked for the company ___for___ 10 years.

2. Sharon has been a teacher _____ 1990.

Present Perfect: *Ever* and *Never*

- We can use *ever* and *never* with the present perfect. We use *ever* in questions. We put *ever* between the subject and the past participle. *Ever* means at any time up to now.
- We use *never* to give negative answer in a sentence. It comes between the verb *have/has* and the past participle. *Never* means at no time up to now.

Q: Have you **ever** been to Seoul?
A: No, I've **never** been to Korea.

Have/Has	Subject	*Ever*	Past Participle	
Have	you	**ever**	eaten	Korean food?

Subject	Have/Has	*Never*	Past Participle	
She	has	**never**	eaten	Korean food.

A Write sentences using the time expressions in brackets, as in the example.

1. You have been to Canada.

   (ever)   *Have you ever been to Canada?*

   (never)   *I have never been to Canada.*

2. Kevin has worked in an office.

   (ever)   _____

   (never)   _____

Have Gone (To) vs. Have Been (To)

Q: Can I speak to Olivia, please?
A: She isn't at home. She **has gone to** the library.

Q: Where **have** you **been**, Olivia?
A: I **have been to** the library.

- She *has gone to* the library. (This means that she hasn't come back yet. She is still at the library.)
- I *have been to* the library. (This means that she has visited the library; she is not there now. She has come back.)

Ⓐ Complete the sentences with *gone* or *been*.

1. Q: Where is Jenny? A: She has ___gone___ to the supermarket.

2. Have you ever _____ to the United States?

3. Alex isn't in his office. I think he has _____ to the bank.

4. Q: Have you _____ to the new restaurant? A: Yes, it is expensive.

Learn & Practice 4

Present Perfect: *Already, Yet,* and *Just*

- We use *already* to emphasize that something happened before now, or before it was expected to happened. *Already* comes before the past participle.
- We use *just* when something happened a short time ago. *Just* comes before the past participle.
- We use *yet* in negative sentences to say that an action we expected hasn't happened, but we think it will. *Yet* comes at the end of the sentence.
- We also use *yet* in questions to ask about something that we expect to happen.

They have **just** got married.

They have **already** had a ceremony.

Q: Have they gone on their honeymoon **yet**?

A: No, they haven't gone on their honeymoon **yet**.

Ⓐ Make sentences using the present perfect tense.

1. the plane / not arrive / yet → _The plane hasn't arrived yet._

2. Clara / eat / dinner / already → _____

3. she / receive / a letter / from her daughter / just → _____

4. they / arrive / yet / ? → _____

5. Nicole / start / her new job / yet / ? → _____

6. the children / go / to bed / already → _____

7. he / bought / a new smartphone / just → _____

A Look at the pictures and prompts and write sentences. Use the present perfect with *for* or *since*.

1.

Ava is a teacher.
she / teach / English / six years

→ She has taught English for six years.

2.

Tom's hobby is collecting stamps.
he / collect / stamps / two years

→ _____

3.

Sarah and Adam work for the company.
they / work / for the company / 1999

→ _____

4.

It rains everywhere.
it / rain / everywhere / last night

→ _____

B Julie has many jobs to do at home this weekend. Write what she has '*already*' done or not '*yet*' done.

1. clean the bedroom (X)   2. take the dog for a walk (O)
3. clean the floor (X)   4. read the magazine (O)
5. wash the dishes (X)   6. wash her car (O)
7. water the plants (X)   8. do the shopping (O)
9. finish her work (O)   10. fix her bicycle (X)

1. She hasn't cleaned the bedroom yet.   2. She has already taken the dog for a walk.

3. _____   4. _____

5. _____   6. _____

7. _____   8. _____

9. _____   10. _____

C Make questions and answers. Use *ever* or *never* as in the example.

1.

Q: *Have you ever seen a humming bird?*

It's the world smallest bird.

A: *No, I haven't. I have never seen a humming bird.*

you / see a humming bird / ?

2.

Q: _____

It's one of the longest 19th-century novels.

A: _____

you / read / *War and Peace* / ?

3.

Q: _____

It's one of the hottest places in the world.

A: _____

you / take a trip / to the Sahara Desert / ?

D Read the sentences and write sentences as in the example. Use the present perfect with *since* or *for*.

1. I first met Chloe in 2008. Chloe and I are still good friends.

→ *Chloe and I have been good friends since 2008.*

2. Jennifer began to live in Seoul five months ago. She still lives there.

→ _____

3. Alan read two history books last Monday. He still reads them.

→ _____

4. They got married in 2007. They are still married.

→ _____

E Complete the sentences with *have/has been (to)* or *have/has gone (to)*.

1. Q: Where are Bob and Nancy? A: They ___*have gone to*___ the theater.

2. I don't live in Seattle. I _____ only _____ there once.

3. Q: Is Brian at home? A: No, he _____ work.

4. Katie has just come home. She _____ the movie theater.

A Look at the example and practice with a partner. Use the words below or invent your own. (Then change roles and practice again.)

1.

How long have you been in this class?

I have been in this class since February.

1.
you / be / in this class / ?
→ February

2.
Cindy / study / English / ?
→ five years

3.
she / have / her driving licence / ?
→ two years

4.
you / work here / ?
→ May

5.
Jessica / have / a bad cold
→ almost a week

6.
they / live in this apartment / ?
→ last year

B Work with a parter. First ask and answer questions about Bill and Mary and then about each other.

	Bill	Mary	You
catch / a big fish	√	✗	
fly / in a plane	✗	√	
travel / abroad	√	✗	
ride / a camel	√	✗	
hold a snake	✗	√	
meet a millionaire	√	✗	

Has Bill ever caught a big fish?

Yes, he has.

Have you ever caught a big fish?

No, I haven't.
I've never caught a big fish.

• Read and answer the questions.

1. Has Harry been to Egypt?

2. What country have Harry been in?

3. Have you ever tried wakeboarding?

Unit Focus

▶ Present Perfect vs. Simple Past: Forms

▶ Present Perfect vs. Simple Past: Meaning

▶ Using *Since*

Fred: Hey Harry, where have you been? I haven't seen you around since June!

Harry: Well, a month ago my family and I went to Italy and we visited my grandparents.

Fred: Did you have a good time?

Harry: Yes, it was great. I tried wakeboarding for the first time.

Learn & Practice 1

Present Perfect vs. Simple Past: Forms

- To form the *simple past*, we add *-ed* or *-d* to the base form of the verb.

- We use the form of *have (has)* + past participle for the present perfect.

Present Perfect	**Simple Past**

Will and Stacey **have been** friends for six years.	Dave and Jeremy **were** friends three years **ago**. Thet **met** by accident **yesterday**.

Time Expressions	**Time Expressions**
ever, before, never, just, how long since, for, already, yet, so far	ago, yesterday, in 1999 last night/week/month/year, etc.

A Complete the sentences as in the example.

1. They ___*have worked*___ (work) there since 2011.

2. We _____ (see) the movie last night.

3. She _____ (make) a great cake yesterday.

4. I _____ (finish) my work two hours ago.

5. _____ (Nicole / start) her new job yet?

Present Perfect vs. Simple Past: Meaning

- We use the present perfect for an action or situation that happened at some unspecified time in the past. The specific time is unimportant, and we cannot state it. The present perfect has an effect in the present.
- We use the simple past to talk about actions and situations that began and ended in the past. We can state the specific time of the action.

Simple Past	Present Perfect
• an action which happened at a stated time in the past	• an action which happened at an unstated indefinite time in the past

They **bought** the house *ten years ago*. (When? Ten years ago. The specific time is mentioned.)	Alicia **has** *already* **bought** a new car. (When? We don't know. The specific time isn't mentioned.)
• an action which started and finished in the past	• an action which started in the past and is still continuing into the present

Jenny **was** a news anchor for 5 years. (She's not a news anchor anymore.)	Ava **has been** a news anchor for 5 years. (She started working as a news anchor 5 years ago and she still is.)

Ⓐ Read and choose the correct words.

1. She (finished / has finished) her homework yesterday.

2. Did you (see / seen) the movie last Saturday?

3. Jamie (visited / has visited) Tokyo before.

4. They (saw / have seen) a ghost twice.

5. Kelly (had / has have) a headache for three hours this morning.

B Complete the sentences with the present perfect or the simple past of the verbs in brackets.

1. Tim and I are good friends. We ____have known____ (know) each other for 10 years.

2. She _____ (go) to Turkey in July, 2008.

3. I have never _____ (eat) such a delicious food.

4. We _____ (live) in Singapore last year.

5. We _____ (live) in Singapore since last year.

Learn & Practice 3

Using Since

- We use the present perfect + since + the simple past to indicate when an action which started in the past and continues up to the present.

I've **studied** English **since** I was an elementary school student.

Our teacher **has given** three tests **since** the semester **began**.

Subject	Past Participle	Since	Subject	Simple Past
Olivia	has studied Chinese	since	she	was a student.

Subject	Simple Past	When	Subject	Simple Past
Olivia	studied Chinese	when	she	was a student.

B Complete the sentences. Use the present perfect or the simple past.

1. When she ____came____ (come) home, it began to snow.

2. I have lived here since I ____was____ (be) a child.

3. My brother got his first skateboard when he _____ (be) 12 years old.

4. Alice _____ (meet) many people since she came here.

5. Kelly _____ (work) at the hotel when she finished school.

6. Sue has had a lot of problems since she _____ (come) to this country.

A Look at the pictures and prompts. Make questions and answers. Use the present perfect or the simple past.

1.

Bill / break / his leg / ?
→ Yes / his leg / last week

Q: Has Bill broken his leg?

A: Yes, he has. He broke his leg last week.

2.

they / ever / visit / Egypt / ?
→ Yes / Egypt / two months ago

Q: _____

A: _____

3.

you / ever / see / the Colosseum / ?
→ Yes / it / on TV / last night

Q: _____

A: _____

4.

you / ever / eat / Korean food / ?
→ Yes / Korean food / yesterday

Q: _____

A: _____

5.

Jason / try / waterskiing / ?
→ Yes / waterskiing / last month

Q: _____

A: _____

6.

Mary / see / a ghost / ?
→ Yes / a ghost / yesterday

Q: _____

A: _____

B Use the prompts to write sentences as in the example. Use the present perfect + *since* + the simple past.

1. My sister / not have / any accidents   she / buy / a new car
   → My sister hasn't had any accidents since she bought a new car.

2. Steve / travel abroad / many times   he / start / working
   → _____

3. Jenny / lose / ten kilos   she / join / a health club
   → _____

4. I / not see / Sheryl   she / move / to Australia
   → _____

C Look at the table below and write sentences. Use the present prefect or the simple past as in the examples.

Henry	buy / a gift for Lisa	O	yesterday
Bob	lock / the door	X	
Bill	prepare for / dinner	X	
The man	repair / our computer	O	on Friday
My father	paint / our house	O	last month
Olivia and Brian	plant / any vegetables / in their garden	X	
Jennifer	buy / the smartphone	O	last night

1. Henry has already bought a gift for Lisa. He bought it yesterday.

2. Bob hasn't locked the door yet.

3. _____

4. _____

5. _____

6. _____

7. _____

A Look at the example and practice with a partner. Use the words below or invent your own. (Then change roles and practice again.)

I.

 Have you ever traveled abroad? Yes, I have.

 Where did you travel? I traveled to Hawaii.

I.

you / ever / travel abroad / ?
where / to Hawaii

2.

you / buy / T-shirt / lately / ?
where / at the shopping mall

3.

you / do your homework / yet / ?
when / last night

4.

you / ever / have a pet / ?
what / a cat

B Work with a partner. Ask and answer questions, using the present perfect and the simple past.

A: Have you ever been to Spain?
B: No, I haven't, but I've been to Italy.
A: Oh really? And when did you go there?
B: I think it was three years ago.

Your turn to ask!

Spain (X)　　Italy (O)
　　　　three years ago

Libya (X)　　Egypt (O)　　USA (X)　　China (O)　　India (X)　　Portugal (O)
　　　　two years ago　　　　four years ago　　　　five years ago

Unit 15 Comparison 1

- Read and answer the questions.
1. What are the girls doing now?
2. Is Jenny older than Jessica?
3. Is Jessica's hair longer than Jenny's?
4. Compare yourself to another person.

Unit Focus

▶ *The Same (As), Similar (To), and Different (From)*

▶ Comparatives

▶ *As...As and Not As...As*

Jenny and Jessica are twins. Jenny is as old as Jessica, but Jenny is taller than Jessica. They have the same smartphones. Jenny's smartphone is the same as Jessica's.

Learn & Practice 1

The Same (As), Similar (To), and Different (From)

- We can show that two things are equal in some way by using *the same (as)* and *the same + noun + as*.
- We use *similar* and *similar to* to say that two things are different in small ways.
- We show that two things are not similar at all by using *different* and *different from*.
- *The same, similar,* and *different* are used as adjectives.

Photo A Photo B	Photo A Photo B	Photo A Photo B
Photos A and B are **the same**. A is **the same as** B. A has **the same** shape **as** B.	Photos A and B are **similar**. A is **similar to** B.	Photos A and B are **different**. A is **different from** B.

A Complete the sentences with *as, to, from, same, similar,* or *different.*

1. My class is the same ___as___ yours.

2. My class is different _____ yours.

3. Gold is similar _____ silver.

4. This car isn't the same price _____ that car.

5. Ava is _____ from her brother.

6. This book is the _____ as that one.

7. This book is _____ to that one.

8. An orange is different _____ a grapefruit.

Comparatives

- When we compare two people, animals, or things, we use the comparative form + *than*. An adjective and an adverb in the comparative form are usually followed by the word *than*.

Short Adjective/Adverb + *-er* Than	More + Longer Adjective + *Than* / More + *-ly* Adverb + *Than*

A cheetah is fast**er than** a tiger. A tiger is strong**er than** a cheetah.	A tiger moves **more** *slowly* **than** a cheetah. A tiger is **more** *dangerous* **than** a cheetah.

	Adjective	Comparative	Adjective	Comparative
Adjective + *-er*	tall small larg**e**	tall**er** small**er** larg**er**	slow short cheap	slow**er** short**er** cheap**er**
Double Consonant	b**ig** f**at**	big**ger** fat**ter**	th**in** h**ot**	thin**ner** hot**ter**
drop *-y* + *-ier*	eas**y** prett**y**	eas**ier** prett**ier**	heav**y** happ**y**	heav**ier** happ**ier**
For most 2 or more syllable adjectives, *more* is used.	famous interesting	**more** famous **more** interesting	expensive difficult	**more** expensive **more** difficult

	Adverb	Comparative	Adverb	Comparative
More is used with adverbs that end in *-ly*.	slowly loudly	**more** slowly **more** loudly	quickly beautifully	**more** quickly **more** beautifully
Adverb + *-er*	fast late	fast**er** lat**er**	hard	hard**er**

	Adjective	Comparative	Adverb	Comparative
Irregular	good bad	**better** **worse**	well badly	**better** **worse**

Ⓐ Complete the sentences with the comparative form of the words in brackets.

1. A bicycle is _____*quieter than*_____ (quiet) a car.

2. A basketball is _____ (big) a baseball.

3. A plane is _____ (fast) a train.

4. This summer is _____ (hot) than last year.

5. Physics is _____ (difficult) history to me.

6. Scott drives _____ (carefully) her.

7. You look _____ (good) your picture.

Learn & Practice 3

As...As and Not As...As

- We can show that two things or people are the similar/same in some way by using *as* + adjective/adverb + *as*.
- We use *not as...as* to show that two things or people are different in some way.
- When we use *not as...as* instead of the comparative, it sometimes sounds more polite.

Steve   Jordan

Steve and Jordan are twins.

Steve is **as** old **as** Jordan. (They are the same age.)
Steve is **as** tall **as** Jordan. (They are the same height.)
Steve is **more** handsome **than** Jordan.
= Jordan **isn't as** handsome **as** Steve. (more polite)

Ⓐ Complete the sentences with *as...as* or *not as...as*.

1. My mother is _____*as old as*_____ (old) my father.

2. Anna is _____ (tall) her sister.

3. Mexico is _____ (not / big) Canada.

4. Soda pop is _____ (not / healthy) fruit juice.

5. Seoyoon can speak English _____ (well) me.

6. The weather today is _____ (cloudy) the weather yesterday.

A Write the sentences about Jenny and Olivia. Compare and answer the questions as in the example.

Jenny

52 kilos
162 centimeters
13 years old

Olivia

35 kilos
140 centimeters
10 years old

1. Q: Is Jenny younger than Olivia?

   A: No, she isn't. Olivia is younger than Jenny.

2. Q: Is Olivia taller than Jenny?

   A: _____

3. Q: Is Olivia heavier than Jenny?

   A: _____

4. Q: Is Jenny shorter than Olivia?

   A: _____

5. Q: Is Olivia older than Jenny?

   A: _____

B Write sentences with *not as...as* and the comparative.

1. Mexico City / London / expensive / crowded

   → Mexico City isn't as expensive as London, but it is more crowded.

2. city life / village life / easy / exciting

   → _____

3. the Gyeongbu Expressway / the country road / interesting / fast

   → _____

4. traveling by plane / traveling by train / cheap / comfortable

   → _____

5. compact cars / medium-sized passenger cars / comfortable / easy to park

   → _____

C Compare the two things or people using the following adjectives.

1.

Compare *Avatar* and *Harry Potter* using "interesting".

→ Avatar is more interesting than Harry Potter. [or]
  Harry Potter is more interesting than Avator.

2.

Compare *Avatar* and *Matrix* using "new".

→ _____
  _____

3.

Compare Bill Gates and Barack Obama using "rich".

→ _____
  _____

4.

Compare Korea and Japan using "large".

→ _____
  _____

D Rewrite each sentence with *not as...as*, but keep the same meaning.

1. Winter is colder than fall.   → Fall is not as cold as winter. _____

2. Days in summer are longer than days in winter.   → _____

3. The apple is smaller than the melon.   → _____

4. Nick speaks more slowly than Stuart.   → _____

E Look at the pictures. Complete the sentences with *same (as)*, *similar (to)*, or *different (from)*.

| Photo A | Photo B | Photo C | Photo D |

1. Photo C and Photo D are ___the same___ .   2. Photo B and Photo C are _____ .

3. Photo C is _____ _____ Photo B.   4. Photo D is _____ _____ Photo C.

5. Photo A and Photo C are _____ .   6. Photo A is _____ _____ Photo B.

A Look at the example and practice with a partner. Use the words below or invent your own. (Then change roles and practice again.)

1.

  Is Korea as big as China?

  No, Korea isn't as big as China. China is bigger than Korea.

1. Korea / big / China / ?
→ No / China

2. the Han River / long / the Nile / ?
→ No / the Nile

3. Korean / difficult / English / ?
→ No / English

4. the Atlantic Ocean / deep /
the Pacific Ocean / ?
→ No / the Pacific Ocean

5. the earth / heavy / the sun / ?
→ No / the sun

6. Mexican food / spicy / Korean
food / ?
→ No / Korean food

B Work with a partner. Compare yourself to another person. Take turns to make sentences using the following adjectives.

I'm not as smart as my brother. He is smarter than me.

Your turn now!

old   patient   religious

talkative   educated   lazy   friendly

athletic   tall   intelligent   smart

strong   interested in sports   pretty

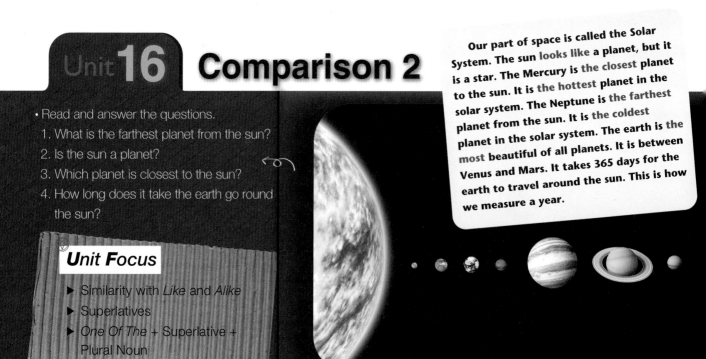

Our part of space is called the Solar System. The sun looks like a planet, but it is a star. The Mercury is the closest planet to the sun. It is the hottest planet in the solar system. The Neptune is the farthest planet from the sun. It is the coldest planet in the solar system. The earth is the most beautiful of all planets. It is between Venus and Mars. It takes 365 days for the earth to travel around the sun. This is how we measure a year.

• Read and answer the questions.
1. What is the farthest planet from the sun?
2. Is the sun a planet?
3. Which planet is closest to the sun?
4. How long does it take the earth go round the sun?

Unit Focus

▶ Similarity with *Like* and *Alike*
▶ Superlatives
▶ *One Of The* + Superlative + Plural Noun

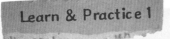

Learn & Practice 1

Similarity with *Like* and *Alike*

- *Like* and *alike* have the same meaning. *Like* is a preposition. It means similar to. *Alike* is an adjective. It means similar.
- We often use the sense perception verbs (*look, sound, smell, taste, feel,* and *seem*) with *like* and *alike*. We can also use other verbs with *like*: *act like, sing like, dress like,* etc.
- We can also show that two things are similar (or not) in internal characteristics with *be like* and *be alike*.

A soccer player **looks like** a rugby player.   The daughter **is like** the mother.
A soccer player and a rugby player **look alike**.   The mother and daughter **are alike**.
(Use *look like* to describe physical appearance.)   (Use *be like* to describe an internal characteristic.)

A Complete the sentences with *like* or *alike*.

1. You look ___like___ your sister.

2. Most four-year-olds act _____.

3. Tom looks _____ Mike.

4. Tom and Mike look _____.

5. A soccer player doesn't dress _____ a football player.

6. It sounds _____ thunder.

7. A rugby player and a football player doesn't dress _____.

Superlatives

- When we compare three or more people or things, we use the superlative form of adjectives and adverbs. We use the definite article *the* before superlative adjectives and adverbs.
- After superlatives, we often use *in* before the names of places such as the world, countries, and cities; and with group nouns such as the class, my family, and the group.
- After superlatives, we often use *of* before expressions of time and quantity, and plural nouns.

Superlative: *-est*	Superlative: *Most*

Antarctica is **the coldest** place **in** the world.	Soccer is the most popular **sport in the world**.

Spelling rules of the superlative forms

	Adjective	Comparative	Superlative
one-syllable adjectives + *-(e)st*	tall large cheap long	tall**er** larg**er** cheap**er** long**er**	the tall**est** the larg**est** the cheap**est** the long**est**
double consonant + *-est*	big hot thin	big**ger** hot**ter** thin**ner**	the big**gest** the hot**test** the thin**nest**
drop *-y* + *-iest*	easy heavy pretty happy	eas**ier** heav**ier** prett**ier** happ**ier**	the eas**iest** the heav**iest** the prett**iest** the happ**iest**
For most two or more syllable adjectives, *most* is used.	difficult famous popular interesting	**more** difficult **more** famous **more** popular **more** interesting	the **most** difficult the **most** famous the **most** popular the **most** interesting

	Adverb	Comparative	Superlative
Most is used with adverbs that end in *-ly*.	carefully beautifully	**more** carefully **more** beautifully	the **most** carefully the **most** beautifully
Adverb + *-est*	hard fast	hard**er** fast**er**	the hard**est** the fast**est**

	Adjective (Adverb)	Comparative	Superlative
Irregular	good (well) bad/ill (badly) many/much little	**better** **worse** **more** **less**	**the best** **the worst** **the most** **the least**

A Complete the sentences with the superlative form of the words in brackets.

1. Summer is ___the hottest___ (hot) of all.

2. The blue whale is _____ (big) of all animals.

3. This is the _____ (comfortable) of all.

4. Kevin is _____ (tall) of the three.

5. Toronto is _____ (large) city in Canada.

B Complete the sentences with *in* or *of*.

1. Kristen is the best driver __in__ her family.

2. Cheetahs run the fastest _____ all the animals.

3. Steve is the tallest _____ all the students.

4. What's the highest mountain _____ Korea?

Learn & Practice 3

One Of The + Superlative + Plural Noun
- We often use *one of the* before a superlative form.

Pollution is **one of the most** serious problems.

Mt. McKinley is **one of the highest** mountains in the world.

	One Of	**Superlative**	**Plural Noun**	
It is She is Seoul is	one of	the biggest the prettiest the most crowded	restaurants girls cities	in the city. in the class. in the world.

A Complete the sentences as in the example. Use *one of* + the superlative form.

1. The wedding ceremony is ___one of the most important ceremonies___ (important ceremony) in life.

2. Jenny is _____ (good student) in her school.

3. Seoul is _____ (big city) in the world.

4. It is _____ (popular site) in Seoul.

A Look at the pictures and prompts. Write sentences with the comparative and superlative forms of the adjectives.

1. the soccer ball / the baseball (small)
   → *The baseball is smaller than the soccer ball.* _____

2. the baseball / the golf ball (big)
   → _____

3. the soccer ball / of the tree (big)
   → _____

4. the golf ball / of all (small)
   → _____

B Look at the pictures and write sentences. Use the prompts and the comparative and superlative forms or *as...as*.

| Hotel A built in 1985 | Hotel B built in 1991 | Hotel C built in 2003 | Hotel D built in 1991 |

1. Hotel A / old / four   → *Hotel A is the oldest of the four.* _____

2. Hotel B / old / Hotel D   → _____

3. Hotel D / old / Hotel C   → _____

4. Hotel C / new / Hotel A   → _____

5. Hotel C / new / four   → _____

C Make sentences as in the example. Use the given phrases and *one of the* + superlative + plural noun.

1. a serious problem in Korea
   → Yellow dust ___is one of the most serious problems in Korea___ .

2. an attractive athlete in the world
   → Kim Yuna _____ .

3. a beautiful building in the world
   → The Taj Mahal _____ .

4. a famous painting in the world
   → Leonardo da Vinci _____ .

D Make sentences with the words given as in the example.

1. Kevin and William have similar faces.
   → Kevin's face is like William's face. _____ Kevin's face / William's face (like)
   → Their faces are alike. _____ their faces (alike)

2. Jenny and Jane have similar names.
   → _____ Jenny's name / Jane's name (like)
   → _____ their names (alike)

3. Carly and Eddie have similar cars.
   → _____ Carly's car / Eddie's car (like)
   → _____ their cars (alike)

E Look at the given words. Choose and write sentences. Use the superlative form.

1. poisonous / snake / world

   rattlesnake?   boa?   python?

   → I think the rattlesnake is the most
   poisonous snake in the world.

2. large / country / world

   China?   Russia?   Canada?

   → _____
   _____

3. fast / animal / world

   zebra?   cheetah?   tiger?

   → _____
   _____

4. popular / sport / Australia

   soccer?   cricket?   baseball?

   → _____
   _____

A Look at the example and practice with a partner. Use the words below or invent your own. (Then change roles and practice again.)

I.

 What is the biggest of all animals?

 I think the blue whale is the biggest of all animals.

1.

big / of all animals / ?
→ the blue whale

2.

tall animal / in the world / ?
→ the giraffe

3.

big bird / in the world / ?
→ the ostrich

4.

far planet / from the sun / ?
→ Pluto

B Work with a partner. You and your partner have recently visited three different restaurants. Look at the information below and make comparisons, as in the example.

Restaurant A

Restaurant B

Restaurant C

	Restaurant A	Restaurant B	Restaurant C
large	★	★★	★★★
expensive	★★★	★★	★
healthy	★★★	★	★★
convenient	★	★★	★★★
crowded	★★	★	★★★

Restaurant B is larger than Restaurant A.

Restaurant C is the most crowded of all (or the three).

A Look at the prompts and write sentences as in the example. Use the present perfect + *since* + the simple past.

1. I / not see / Jessica   she / move / to Korea

    → I haven't seen Jessica since she moved to Korea.

2. I / study / English   I / be / an elementary school student

    → _____

3. Our teacher / give / three tests   the semester / begin

    → _____

B Read and choose the correct words.

1. She (graduated / have graduated) in 2013 from a university.

2. I (took / have taken) this medicine for two weeks now and I already feel much better.

3. This is my favorite store. I (shopped / have shopped) here many times.

4. Sarah (gave / has given) me this book for my birthday last year.

C Look at the pictures and prompts. Make questions and answers. Use the present perfect or the simple past.

1.  you / every / eat / Korean food / ?   Yes / two years ago

   Q: Have you ever eaten Korean food?

   A: Yes, I have. I ate Korean food two years ago.

2.  Aaron / ever / visit / Rome / ?   Yes / five years ago

   Q: _____

   A: _____

3.  Jennifer / just / buy / a new telescope / ?   No / a new digital camera

   Q: _____

   A: _____

D Complete the sentences with the correct form (positive, comparative, or superlative) of the adjectives/adverbs in brackets.

1. The mouse is not _____*as big as*_____ (big) the dog.

2. The elephant is _____ (heavy) of the three.

3. The dog is _____ (heavy) the mouse.

4. The dog can run _____ (fast) the elephant.

5. The mouse is _____ (small) of them all.

6. The dog is not _____ (small) the mouse.

E Fill in the comparative form as in the example.

1. My motorbike goes _____*faster than*_____ (fast) yours.

2. I work _____ (hard) Eric.

3. Today it is _____ (cold) yesterday.

4. The last bus was _____ (crowded) the first bus.

5. Traveling by train is _____ (expensive) traveling by bus.

F Write sentences using the prompts and *one of the* + superlative + plural noun.

1. Toronto / big city / in Canada
   → *Toronto is one of the biggest cities in Canada.* _____

2. Olivia / intelligent person / in our class
   → _____

3. the Grand Canyon / beautiful place / in the world
   → _____

4. Kim Taehee / pretty actress / in the world
   → _____

5. the Han River / great historical significance / of Korea
   → _____

Unit 17 Gerunds and Infinitives 1

• Read and answer the questions.

1. Why do many people visit Italy?
2. Why does the tower lean?
3. What problem does the tower have today?

Unit Focus

▶ Gerund as Subject and Object
▶ Infinitive as Subject and Object
▶ Verb + Gerund or Infinitive
▶ Infinitive of Purpose / Verb + Object + Infinitive

Have you ever seen the Leaning Tower of Pisa? I went to Italy **to see** the Leaning Tower of Pisa last summer. Every year, many people visit Italy **to see** it. I enjoyed **seeing** the famous tower. Unfortunately it leans because of its poor design and a mistake in its construction. In addition, it is also falling apart like all old buildings. People in Italy want **to save** the tower.

Learn & Practice 1

Gerund as Subject and Object

- To form a *gerund*, we add *-ing* to the base form of the verb. Like a noun or a pronoun, the gerund can be the subject or the object of a sentence. When we use a gerund as the subject, the gerund subject takes a singular verb.
- After certain verbs, we only use a gerund as the object.

Jogging every day *is* good for your health.
Amy *enjoys* **jogging** in the morning.

Verb		Object
enjoy finish give up keep mind avoid stop put off quit dislike	+	**verb + -ing**

(A) Complete the sentences using the prompts given, as in the example.

1. _____Watching TV_____ (watch / TV) all evening is boring, let's do something else.

2. _____ (speak / in English) is hard at first.

3. Would you mind _____ (turn on / the air conditioner)?

4. _____ (swim / in the river) alone is dangerous.

5. _____ (be / on time for school) is important.

6. She finished _____ (do / her homework), and then she went jogging.

Infinitive as Subject and Object

- An infinitive (*to* + the base verb) can act like a noun in a sentence. The infinitive can be the subject or the object of a sentence.
- There is no difference in meaning between an infinitive subject and a gerund subject.
- When we use an infinitive as the subject, we begin the sentence with *it* and delay the infinitive.
- After certain verbs, we have to use an infinitive.

To eat junk food *is* not good for children.
= **It** isn't good for children **to eat** junk food.
Children *want* **to eat** junk food.

Verb		Object
want expect would like need decide plan hope promise refuse seem	+	**to + base verb**

A Rewrite the sentences with the same meaning by using *it* + an infinitive.

1. To have good friends is important. → It is important to have good friends.

2. To study English is very important these days. → _____

3. To get up early is a good habit. → _____

Verb + Gerund or Infinitive

- We can use a gerund or an infinitive after certain verbs. Usually there is no difference in meaning.

It *began* **to rain**.
It *began* **raining**.

like	love	start	continue
hate	can't stand		

∗After *would like*, we use the infinitive and not the gerund.
(I *would like* **to go** to a movie tonight.)

A Complete the sentences with a gerund and an infinitive of each of the verbs given.

1. sing　The girl began ___to sing___ .
　　　　　The girl began ___singing___ .

2. do　Steve hates _____ his homework.
　　　　Steve hates _____ his homework.

3. fight　They started _____ .
　　　　　They started _____ .

4. fly　Does she love _____ kites?
　　　　Does she love _____ kites?

Infinitive of Purpose / Verb + Object + Infinitive

- We use an infinitive to explain the purpose of an action. It often answers the questions why. In more formal English, we use *in order to* + a base verb to explain a purpose.
- We can also use *for* to show purpose. We use a noun after *for*.

Ava wanted some books, so she went to the bookstore.
→ She *went* to the bookstore **to buy** some books.
→ She *went* to the bookstore **in order to buy** some books.
→ She *went* to the bookstore **for** some books.

- After certain verbs, we use the verb + an object + an infinitive. We often say that we want somebody to do something.

The doctor **advised** Holly **to exercise** every day.

Verb		Infinitive
advise, allow, ask, encourage, order, want (or would like), persuade, permit, teach, tell, warn	+ **Object** +	to + base verb

A Complete the sentences with *to* or *for*.

1. I went to the store ___to___ buy a newspaper.
2. They're going to Brazil _____ a holiday.
3. She went to the station _____ catch a train.
4. We went to the restaurant _____ lunch.

B Put the words in brackets into the correct form.

1. They didn't want _____ *anybody to know* _____ (anybody / know) their secret.

2. She expects _____ (I / work) at night and on weekends.

3. The doctor advised _____ (Jessica / eat) more vegetables.

4. The captain ordered _____ (his crew / leave) the ship immediately.

A Use the prompts to answer the questions below, as in the example.

1.

Why do they recycle old newspapers and magazines? (protect / the environment)

They recycles old newspapers and magazines to protect the environment.

2.

Why did Claire call Liam yesterday? (invite him / to her party)

_____

_____

3.

Why did Jason put on his sportswear? (go jogging)

_____

_____

4.

Why is Lindsay going to Pizza Hut tonight? (have dinner / with Eric)

_____

_____

B Read the dialogs and complete the sentences. Use an object + an infinitive.

1.

OK. / Can you help me?

She wanted *him (or the man) to help her*.

2.

Can I use your dictionary? / No.

One girl wouldn't allow _____ _____.

3.

You should exercise every day. / OK.

The doctor told _____ _____.

4.

Be careful! / Don't worry. I will.

She warned _____.

C Make sentences to describe the pictures as in the example. Use gerund subjects.

1.

fly in an airplane /
not dangerous

Flying in an airplane isn't dangerous.

2.

learn foreign
languages /
interesting

_____

3.

walk alone at night /
dangerous

_____

4.

watch TV for too
long /
bad for your eyes

_____

D Complete the sentences using the prompts provided. Use the infinitive.

1. likes / play computer games
   → She ___likes to play computer games___ .

2. want / see a scary movie
   → Tony _____ .

3. be planning / go to Korea next week
   → I _____ .

4. started / talk about her problem
   → Molly _____ .

E Rewrite the sentences with the same meaning by using an infinitive as the subject.

1. It is easy to ride a bicycle.   → To ride a bicycle is easy.

2. It's not difficult to learn Korean.   → _____

3. It is very hard these days to get a good job.   → _____

4. It's not easy to live in a foreign country.   → _____

F Look at the table and complete the sentences.

	play computer games	learn Japanese
Natalie	refuse	plan
Kimberly	want	promise
Derek	enjoy	finish

1. Natalie refuses ___playing computer games___ . She planned ___to learn Japanes___ .

2. Kimberly wants _____ . She promised _____ yesterday.

3. Derek enjoys _____ every day. He finished _____ .

A Look at the example and practice with a partner. Use the words below or invent your own. (Then change roles and practice again.)

I.

 What do you enjoy when you have free time?

 I enjoy traveling around the country. How about you?

 I like reading novels.

1.  enjoy / travel around the country
→ like / read novels

2.  enjoy / watch a horror movie
→ like / listen to K-pop music

3.  enjoy / go to archaeological museums
→ like / climb rocks

4.  enjoy / try Korean food
→ like / watch sitcoms

B Work with a partner. Read about Cory and Joel. Then in pairs ask and answer questions as in the example.

	Cory	Joel
LIKE	make model planes	go scuba diving
DISLIKE	study Japanese	wake up early
WANT TO BE	a doctor	a photographer
WOULD LIKE	try mountain biking	try canoeing
HOPE	go camping	go to a foreign country alone

What does Cory like doing?

She likes making model planes.

C Now complete the table below about you. Ask questions to find out information about your partner as in the example. Finally, compare you and your partner.

	YOU	YOUR PARTNER
LIKE		
DISLIKE		
WANT TO BE		
WOULD LIKE		
HOPE		

What do you like doing?

I like...

Unit **18** Gerunds and Infinitives 2

- Read and answer the questions.
1. Are you looking forward to going on holiday?
2. What are you interested in?
3. Would you like to go swimming?
4. Are you used to living in your town?

Unit Focus

▶ Preposition + Gerund / *Go* + -*ing*
▶ Adjective + infinitive
▶ *Be Used To* + Gerund
▶ Using Infinitives with *Too* and *Enough*

Are you looking for a wonderful place **to spend** your holiday? Then you should visit Golden Sea Hotel. Some people want **to relax** or other people are just looking forward to **having** exciting holiday. You'll be surprised **to find** out how many things you can do there. You can **go swimming** in the sea or in the pool. You can enjoy **exercising** in the gym and tennis courts. Don't you think that July is **too late to go** on holiday? We advise you **to ask** your travel agent for our special prices for July.

Learn & Practice 1

Preposition + Gerund / *Go* + -*ing*

- When we use a verb after a preposition, we must use the verb in the *gerund (-ing form)*. The *gerund* is the object of the preposition.

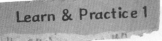

I'm tired **of doing** the same thing every day.

Prepositions following Verbs/Adjectives		
fond **of**	worry **about**	interested **in**
apologize **for**	insist **on**	believe **in**
care **about**	succeed **in**	think **about**
good **at**	tired **of**	excited **about**
feel **like**	responsible **for**	look forward **to**

- We use a gerund after the verb *go* to express recreational activities. There is no *to* between *go* and the gerund.

Sophia **went** swimm**ing** yesterday.
She **goes** shopp**ing** once a week.

Go		**-ing**	
go	+	camp**ing**	fish**ing**
		shopp**ing**	hik**ing**
		jogg**ing**	bowl**ing**
		sightsee**ing**	sail**ing**
		skat**ing**	swimm**ing**

A Read and circle the correct form.

1. She is proud of (to be / being) a nurse.   2. I'm thinking about (going / to go) on a diet.

3. Are you interested in (to watch / watching) TV?   4. She came here (to learn / learning) English.

B Look at the pictures and complete the sentences. Use *go* + *-ing*.

1.

Do you ___*go skiing*___ every winter?

ski

2.

We _____ last week.

camp

Adjective + Infinitive

- We can use adjective + infinitive to say what we think of things that people do.
- We can also use infinitives after adjectives for feelings, like *afraid*, *glad*, *pleased*, *happy*, *sad*, *surprised*, *amazed*, *frightened*, *disappointed*, *wrong*, *sorry*, *touched*.

Japanese is *difficult* to **understand**.

We were *touched* **to watch** the movie.

A Combine the two sentences to make one, using an adjective + an infinitive.

1. We were lucky. + We could get tickets. → *We were lucky to get tickets.*

2. I was very delighted. + I won the lottery. → _____

Be Used To + Gerund

- We use *be used to* + gerund to talk about something that we are familiar with because we have done it often. *Be used to* and *be accustomed to* have the same meaning.
- Do not confuse *be used to* + gerund with *used to* + base verb. We use *used to* + base verb to talk about past habits or things that do not happen anymore.

I'm not **used to** eating with a knife and fork.
I'm accustomed to eating with chopsticks.

Ava **used to** wash clothes by hand.
Now she doesn't.

A Complete the sentences with *be used to* or *used to* and the verbs in brackets.

1. Gina is an actress. She ___is used to wearing___ (wear) expensive clothes.

2. They _____ (be) very good friends, but now they hate each other.

3. Ron is a taxi driver. He _____ (drive) for long hours.

4. Kathy left her parents' house two years ago. Now she _____ (do) the housework.

5. I _____ (drink) coffee, but now I prefer drinking tea.

Learn & Practice 4

Using Infinitives with *Too* and *Enough*

- We use *too* + adjective + infinitive. We use *too* in front of an adjective. In the speaker's mind, the use of *too* implies a negative result.
- We use *adjective* + *enough* + infinitive. *Enough* means sufficiently. In the speaker's mind, the use of *enough* implies a positive meaning. It is followed by *to*-infinitive.
- We can also use *enough* + noun. *Enough* comes in front of the noun.

This coffee is **too hot** (for her) **to drink**.

Emma is **tall enough to reach** the top shelf.

They had **enough time to go** to the park.

A Complete the sentences with *too* or *enough* and the adjectives in brackets.

1. A: Can you reach that top shelf?
   B: No, I'm not ___tall enough___ to reach it. (tall)

2. A: Did they go on a picnic yesterday?
   B: No, it was _____ to go on a picnic. (cold)

3. A: Did Sarah enjoy the scary movie?
   B: No, she was _____ to enjoy it. (scared)

4. A: Does William go to school?
   B: No, he isn't _____ to go to school yet. (old)

A Look at the pictures and rewrite the sentences using *too/enough*.

1.

Jake is tired. He can't work.

→ _Jake is too tired to work._

2.

She is strong enough. She can carry the suitcase.

→ _____

3.

Dave was too angry. He couldn't talk to anyone.

→ _____

4.

She is tall enough. She can reach the ceiling.

→ _____

5.

Do you have enough time? You can go to the park.

→ _____

6.

They have enough vegetables. They can make sandwiches.

→ _____

B Combine the two sentences to make one, using an adjective + an infinitive.

1. Brian met his girlfriend at the airport. He was delighted.

   → _Brian was delighted to meet his girlfriend at the airport._

2. Brittany failed the exam three times. She was very ashamed.

   → _____

3. She heard the truth about her boyfriend. She was shocked.

   → _____

4. Eric bought a new sports car yesterday. He was very happy.

   → _____

C Look at the pictures. Read the dialogs and complete the sentences as in the example.

1.
> Did you get the job?
> Yes, I did.

The woman succeeded in _getting the job_ .

2.
> Elena, would you like to learn how to play the guitar?
> Oh, yes, I would.

Elena is interested in _____ _____ .

3.
> Hooray! I'm going on holiday tomorrow!
> Me, too!

John and Maria are looking forward to _____ .

4.
> I am sorry for being so rude yesterday.
> Oh, that's okay.

She apologized for _____ _____ to me.

D Complete the sentences with a form of *go* and a form of the verbs in brackets.

1. Yesterday Shannon visited a department store and bought some T-shirts.
   → Yesterday Shannon _____went shopping_____ . (shop)

2. We take our skis to our favorite mountain resort and enjoy an exciting weekend.
   → We _____ at our favorite mountain resort.

3. William takes his fishing pole to a farm pond every Saturday.
   → William _____ every Saturday.

E Read these situations and write sentences with *be used to*.

1. Alice was born and raised in Chicago.
   (she / used / live / in a big city)   _She is used to living in a big city._

2. Kevin sleeps on the floor. He doesn't mind this. He has always slept on the floor.
   (he / used / sleep / on the floor)   _____

3. Sarah drives on the right. She doesn't mind this. She always drives on the right.
   (she / drive / on the right)   _____

A Look at the example and practice with a partner. Use the words below or invent your own. (Then change roles and practice again.)

I.

 Would you like to go hiking?

 No, I don't like going hiking. I like going fishing.

1.
hiking?
No → fishing

2.
bowling?
No → jogging

3.
skating?
No → skiing

4.
camping?
No → shopping

5.
sightseeing?
No → snowboarding

6.
scuba diving?
No → paragliding

B Work with a partner. Can you do these things? Ask and answer each question with *too* or *enough*. You and your partner may use the adjectives in the box in answers.

1. Can you reach the top shelf?
2. Can you carry a heavy suitcase?
3. Can you fight with a tiger?
4. Can you jump from an airplane?
5. Can you make people laugh?
6. Can you put a whole orange in your mouth at one time?
7. Can you buy a very expensive car?

rich tall
serious
brave short
strong poor
dangerous
weak funny
big small

Can you reach the top shelf?

No, I can't. I'm not tall enough to reach the top shelf. / I'm too short to reach the top shelf.

Unit 19 Conjunctions

• Read and answer the questions.
1. Do you know about Lee Sunsin?
2. Why did his teacher like him?
3. What did he invent?
4. If he were not to defeat the Japanese navy during the Imjin war, what would happen to Korea?

Unit Focus

▶ The Conjunctions: *And, But,* and *Or*
▶ The Conjunctions: *So* and *Because*
▶ *Too, So, Either,* and *Neither*

Admiral Lee Sunsin was a great hero. When Sunsin was young, he was brave and clever. His teacher, who was called "Hunjang," liked him a lot because he learned faster than other boys. He read books for long hours, so he slept for only five or six hours a day. He always practiced how to shoot an arrow and how to fight, but his father disliked his behavior like this. Sunsin always wanted to keep our nation safe and sound, so he prevented our nation against Japanese's invasion with only a few ships.

Learn & Practice 1

The Conjunctions: *And, But,* and *Or*

- We use the conjunction *and* to join sentences that are about similar ideas, actions, or situations. *And* can also join one sentence that gives extra information to the other. We use a comma before *and* when it joins sentences.
- We use the conjunction *but* to give opposite or different ideas. *But* can also join a positive sentence and a negative sentence that talk about the same subject. We use a comma before *but* when it joins sentences.
- We use the conjunction *or* to join sentences that give a choice. We use a comma before *or* when it joins sentences.

She played the piano, **and** I sang a song.

Tom proposed to her, **but** she refused.

You can eat it here, **or** you can take it out.

- When *and, but,* and *or* link two words that are not sentences, we don't use a comma. Commas (,) are used when three or more items are joined. In a series of three or more items, the comma before *and* is optional.
- Do not use a comma when the verb in the second part of the sentence does not have its own subject in that part of the sentence.

We saw lions, alligators, **and** bears.
Nurses must be hard-working **and** patient.
Penguins can swim, **but** they can't fly. (Use a comma.)
Penguins can swim **but** can't fly. (Do not use a comma.)

We saw lions, alligators, **and** bears.
The car is old **but** good.

A Complete the sentences with *and, but,* or *or.* Add commas where necessary.

1. I bought some apples, but I didn't eat them.

2. I met Tom _____ Kelly at the party.

3. The woman is old _____ healthy.

4. I saw a cat, a mouse _____ a puppy.

5. You may go there _____ you may stay here.

6. I wanted to see a doctor _____ saw a nurse.

Learn & Practice 2

The Conjunctions: *So* and *Because*

- We use the conjunction *so* to join two sentences. *So* gives us the result of an action or thought. We must use a comma before *so*.
- We use the conjunction *because* to give a reason for something or to say why something happens. *Because* answers the question *why* in English and is followed by a reason.

It started to rain, **so** she opened her umbrella.

He was very upset **because** I didn't tell the truth.

A Complete the sentences with *so* or *because.* Use commas when necessary.

1. She is very kind, so everyone likes her.

2. I went to see a doctor _____ I was sick.

3. I'm very hungry _____ I didn't eat anything today.

4. The weather was wonderful yesterday _____ we went to the park.

5. My dad couldn't watch the news yesterday _____ the TV was broken.

6. The movie was very long _____ we got home late.

7. I lost my transportation card _____ I couldn't take the bus or the subway.

Too, So, Either, and Neither

- We use *too* and *so* to agree with or add information to affirmative ideas.
- We use *either* and *neither* to agree with or add information to negative ideas.

Janet has straight hair.	**So do I.** = I do too. = Me too.
	= I have straight hair, too.
Janet doesn't have curly hair.	**Neither do I.** = I don't either. = Me neither.
	= I don't have curly hair, either.
Janet is a student.	**So am I.** = I am too. = Me too.
	= I'm a student, too.

Affirmative Statement	Agreement with *Too*		Agreement with *So*		
	Subject + Verb	Too	So	Auxiliary Verb	Subject
I like Jacob.	I do, I like him,			do	I.
I am a student.	I am, I am a student,			am	I.
We are studying.	They are, They are studying,	too.	So	are	they.
Ben went to Seoul.	Mia did, Mia went there,			did	Mia.
Erin can drive.	Adam can, Adam can drive,			can	Adam.

Negative Statement	Agreement with *Either*		Agreement with *Neither*		
	Subject + Verb + *Not*	Either	Neither	Auxiliary Verb	Subject
I'm not hungry.	I'm not, I'm not hungry,			am	I.
I don't like baseball.	Kevin doesn't, Kevin doesn't like it,			does	Kevin.
I didn't enjoy the movie.	They didn't, They didn't enjoy it,	either	Neither	did	they.
They won't go.	We won't, We won't go,			will	we.
I can't do that.	I can't, I can't do it,			can	I.

* **Me too** and **me neither** are often used in informal spoken English.

Ⓐ Write sentences showing agreement using *so* and *neither*. Use *I*.

1. A: I didn't enjoy the movie last night.
   B: ___Neither did I.___

2. A: I'm tired.
   B: _____

3. A: I can speak English very well.
   B: _____

4. A: I won't go to the party.
   B: _____

A Choose the best conjunction to join the sentences.

1. It was very cold. I closed the window. (so / because)

   → It was very cold, so I closed the window.

2. They didn't go for a drive. They didn't have time. (but / because)

   → _____

3. It began to rain. He opened her umbrella. (so / and)

   → _____

4. The weather was cold. We went fishing anyway. (or / but)

   → _____

5. We can go fishing. We can just stay home. (but / or)

   → _____

B Rewrite these sentences as in the example. Use *so* or *neither*.

1. I didn't enjoy the movie last night, and Katie didn't enjoy the move last night.

   → I didn't enjoy the movie last night, and neither did Katie.

2. I don't like salty food, and my wife doesn't like salty food.

   → _____

3. Alex goes to college, and his sisters go to college.

   → _____

4. Brian can't speak Japanese, and I can't speak Japanese.

   → _____

C Write sentences about what you did yesterday. Use the words in brackets.

1. (and)   Yesterday I stayed home and listened to some music.

2. (because) Last night I went to the library because I had to return the library books.

3. (but)   _____

4. (and)   _____

5. (so)   _____

6. (because) _____

D Look at the pictures and prompts. Complete the sentences using *and*, *but*, *so*, or *because*.

1.

open / the window / she

It was very hot, ___so she opened the window___

_____.

2.

CLOSED

be closed / it

They went to the restaurant, _____

_____.

3.

rain / a lot / it

We didn't enjoy our vacation, _____

_____.

4.

television / watch

Last night I stayed at home _____

_____.

E Join the sentences with *because* and with *so*.

1. She passed the exam. She had a good teacher.
   → _She passed the exam because she had a good teacher._____
   → _She had a good teacher, so she passed the exam._____

2. I changed my hotel. The rooms were very dirty.
   → _____
   → _____

3. He didn't buy the jeans. They were expensive.
   → _____
   → _____

F Complete the dialogs by agreeing with Speaker A's idea. Use *so* or *neither*. Use *I*.

1. A: I haven't been here before.
   B: _Neither have I._____

2. A: I always have coffee in the morning.
   B: _____

3. A: My dad served in the military.
   B: _____

4. A: The teacher was late for class.
   B: _____

5. A: I won't come here again.
   B: _____

6. A: I'm not good at making conversation.
   B: _____

A Look at the example and practice with a partner. Use the words below or invent your own. (Then change roles and practice again.)

1.

 Why was Jason hungry?

 He was hungry because there was no food in the house.

1.

Jason / hungry / ?
→ there was no food / in the house

2.

the women / laugh hard / ?
→ the joke / very funny

3.

Jake / fail / the test / ?
→ he / not study

4.

Nancy's family / have / problems / ?
→ Her husband / lose / his job

5.

Chris / angry / ?
→ the music / too loud

6.

Andrew / late / ?
→ he / miss / the bus

B Work with a partner. Take turns to say what type of TV programs you like / don't like.

1. soap operas

2. the news

3. realty shows

4. sports programs

5. wildlife documentaries

6. quiz shows

7. the weather forecast

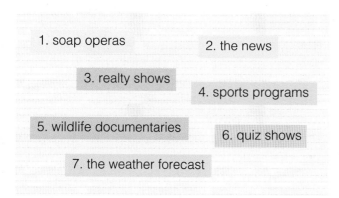

I don't like soap operas.

Neither do I. They're boring.

Conditional Clauses

• Read and answer the questions.
1. What does Sarah wish for?
2. What are you going to do if the weather is nice tomorrow?
3. What would you do to make the world a better place if you were a politician?

Unit *Focus*

▶ Present Real (or Zero) Conditional
▶ First Type (or Future) Conditional Sentences
▶ Second Type Conditional Sentences
▶ Wishes about the Present or Future

Sarah: Jenny, if you don't water these plants, they die.
Kelly: Sarah, if you didn't work in this shop, what would you like to do?
Sarah: Well, I wish I were a rich and famous movie director.
Kelly: Ah, I wish you were a bit more realistic!
Sarah: Why do you say that? If I directed a movie, it would be a huge success.

Learn & Practice 1

Present Real (or Zero) conditional

- We use two clauses in a conditional sentence: an *if-clause* and a main clause. The *if-clause* contains the condition and the *main clause* contains the result.
- We can put the *if-clause* before or after the main clause. There is no difference in meaning. Use a comma (,) after the *if-clause* when it comes at the beginning.
- We use the present real conditional to talk about general facts or things that happen every day or about what happens when there is a definite situation. We use the simple present in both clauses. In present real conditionals, we can use *when* instead of *if*.

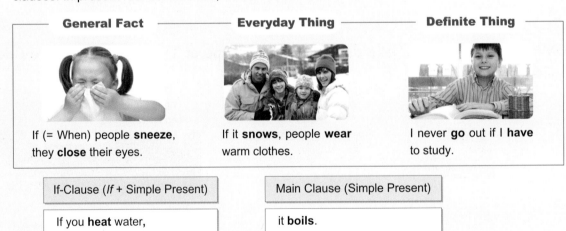

General Fact	Everyday Thing	Definite Thing
If (= When) people **sneeze**, they **close** their eyes.	If it **snows**, people **wear** warm clothes.	I never **go** out if I **have** to study.

If-Clause (*If* + Simple Present)	Main Clause (Simple Present)
If you **heat** water,	it **boils**.

A Complete the sentences, putting the verbs into the correct tense.

1. If you ___exercise___ a lot, you ___lose weight___ . (exercise / lose weight)

2. If the temperature of water _____ to freezing point, it _____ into ice. (drop / turn)

First Type (or Future) Conditional Sentences

- We use future conditional sentences to talk about events or situations that can possibly happen in the present or future.
- We do not use *will* or *be going to* in a conditional clause even though we are talking about the future. We use the simple present in the *if-clause* and the future tense in the main clause.
- In the main clause, we can use any verb form that refers to the future.

If she **gets** the job, she **will buy** a car.	If you **have** a passport, you **can travel** abroad.	He **will catch** a cold if he **goes** out without a coat.

A Complete the sentences using the prompts in brackets as in the example.

1. If you do your homework fast, you ____will make____ (make / will) mistakes.

2. If my sister visits me, we _____ (go / be going to) to the park.

3. If you hurry, you _____ (catch / may) the bus.

Second Type Conditional Sentences

- We use *if* + simple past and *would/could* + base verb to express something which is not very likely to happen in the present or the future. We use a past tense verb in the *if*-clause. But the meaning is not past. We imagine a result in the present or the future.

If I **won** the lottery, I **would buy** you a house.
If I **were** a millionaire, I **would buy** a luxurious house on the hill.

If-Clause			Main Clause		
If	**Subject**	**Past Tense Verb**	**Subject**	**Would/Could**	**Base Verb**
If	I/ you/he/she we/they	**had** a lot of money, **were** very rich,	I/you/he/she we/they	**would/could**	**buy** the house.

- Remember, after if, we use *were* for all persons. We can also use *was* instead of *were* when the subject is *I, he, she, it* or a singular noun. However, we use *were* as a way of giving advice.

A Put the verbs in brackets into the correct form. Is it first or second conditional?

1. If they ___earned___ (earn) more money, they could buy a bigger house. → ___second___

2. If you _____ (study) hard, you will pass the exam. → _____

3. Would Peter mind if I _____ (borrow) his bicycle? → _____

4. If I _____ (be) you, I would go and apologize to her. → _____

5. If she _____ (have) enough time, she will come to the party. → _____

Learn & Practice 4

Wishes about the Present or Future

- We use *wish* + the simple past to make a wish about a present situation which we would like to be different.
- We use *could* after wish to express regret about something we cannot do at present.
- For the verb *be*, we use *were* for most subjects. In informal English, many people use *was* for the subjects *I, he, she,* and *it*.

I **wish** I **knew** Kevin's phone number.

I **wish** I **were** a doctor.

I **wish** I **could go** to Julie's party.

Main Clause		Noun Clause		
Subject	*Wish*	**(That)**	**Subject**	**Past Tense Verb**
I/You/We/They	wish	(that)	I/you/she/he it/we/they	Simple Past / *Were (Was)*
He/She/It	wishes			

A Karen is unhappy. She wishes things were different. Write sentences about what she wishes.

1. "I don't have a car." → *She wishes she had a car.*

2. "My roommate is not nice." → _____

3. "I can't go to Korea for my vacation." → _____

4. "I don't speak French." → _____

5. "Teachers are not friendly." → _____

A What will you see if you and your friends go to the following places? Write sentences using the prompts.

1. Seoul / the Seoul Tower
   → If we go to Seoul, we will see the Seoul Tower.

2. Rome / the Colosseum
   → _____

3. New York / the Statue of Liberty
   → _____

4. Sydney / the Sydney Opera House
   → _____

5. Egypt / the Pyramids
   → _____

B Read the situations and give advice. Use *if I were you* and the prompts given.

wake up / earlier / in the morning	apologize / to him
buy / her a new one	go / on a diet.

1.

   She says, "I've put on 10 kg since Christmas!"
   → If I were you, I would go on a diet.

2.

   He says, "I always miss the bus."
   → _____

3.

   She says, "I was very rude to Seojin this morning."
   → _____

4.

   He says, "Olivia lent me her book last week and I think I've lost it."
   → _____

C Join the sentences to form the present real conditional. Use the words in brackets.

1.

Sometimes the temperature reaches -15°C.
Then, the lake freezes. (if)

→ If the temperature reaches -15°C, the lake

freezes.

2.

I often get lost when I go to the city center.
So, I use my GPS to find my position. (if)

→ _____

_____

3.

Sometimes people are rude and selfish.
These people don't have many friends. (if)

→ _____

_____

4.

People usually recycle plastic bottles. Then,
they protect the environment. (when)

→ _____

_____

D Heather has a bad cold. She has to stay in bed. Read what she says and make sentences, as in the example.

1. I have a fever.
2. I have a sore throat.
3. I want to play outside in the snow, but I can't.
4. I have to take medicine.
5. I have to stay in bed.
6. I can't go to my friend's party tonight.
7. My grandmother isn't here with me.

1. I wish I didn't have a fever.

2. _____

3. _____

4. _____

5. _____

6. _____

7. _____

A Look at the example and practice with a partner. Use the words below or invent your own. (Then change roles and practice again.)

1.

 What would you do if someone called you in the middle of the night?

 If someone called me in the middle of the night, I would wake up and answer the phone.

2.

someone call you in the middle of the night
→ wake up and answer the phone

3.

all the lights suddenly go out
→ get my flashlight and turn it on

4.

you find a snake in your room
→ close the door and get someone to help me remove it

5.

you see a strange person breaking into your neighbor's house
→ call the police

B Work with a partner. Ask and answer questions as in the example.

Nick: to live in a quiet town

What does Nick wish for?

He wishes he lived in a quiet town.

Your turn to ask!

Jack: to take the skateboard everywhere

Isabella: to walk down the beach

Ava: to be slimmer

the children: to go camping

Julie: can speak English better

Steve: my daughter - not ask me for money all the time

A **Complete the sentences with *used to* + base verb or *be used to* + gerund and the verbs in brackets.**

1. My sister has been a nurse for 5 years. She ____is used to working____ (work) at night.

2. I _____ (drink) coffee, but now I prefer drinking green tea.

3. Peter _____ (eat) Kimchi, but it was difficult at the beginning.

4. Olivia doesn't take ballet lessons anymore, but she _____ (take) them three times a week.

5. Ava is a famous actress. She is _____ (sign) autographs.

B **Make sentences using the words provided. Use the infinitive.**

1. She turned up the volume.   why: hear the news better
   → _She turned up the volume to hear the news better._____

2. I called the hotel desk.   why: ask for an extra pillow
   → _____

3. We turned on the radio.   why: listen to the news about the earthquake in Japan
   → _____

4. They want to work overtime.   why: earn more money
   → _____

C **The following are well-known scientific facts or natural laws. Put the verbs into the right form.**

1. If the temperature of water ___drops___ (drop) to freezing point, it ___turns___ (turn) into ice.

2. If we _____ (add) oil and water together, the oil _____ (float) on top.

3. If you _____ (throw) a stone into the air, gravity _____ (pull) it back to the earth again.

4. If a cloud _____ (release) electricity, this _____ (find) the shortest way to the ground.

D **Rephrase the following sentences as suggested below.**

1. You must help me. → I want _____you to help me_____.

2. They must not leave now. → I don't want _____.

3. Jessica must eat her dinner. → I want _____.

E **Combine the two sentences to make one, using an adjective + an infinitive.**

1. Tiffany failed the exam three times. She was very ashamed.
   → Tiffany was ashamed to fail the exam three times. _____

2. My mother heard the bad news. She was very shocked.
   → _____

F **Complete the sentences as in the example. Use prepositions and gerunds.**

1. Steve interrupted me. He apologized for that.
   → Steve apologized _____for interrupting_____ me.

2. I like to watch scary movies. I'm interested in that.
   → I'm interested _____ scary movies.

3. We helped an old woman. She thanked us for that.
   → An old woman thanked us _____ her.

4. Isabella wanted to take a taxi to work. She insisted on that.
   → Isabella insisted _____ a taxi.

5. I'm not a good art student. I try to draw paintings, but I'm not very good at it.
   → I'm not good _____ paintings.

G **Choose a, b, or c to complete the sentences.**

1. If I had a driving licence, I _____ my father's car.

   a. will drive   (b.) could drive   c. drove

2. If Tom _____ to smoke, he must go outside. I can't stand people smoking in here.

   a. will want   b. wants   c. doesn't want

3. If you heat ice, it _____ .

   a. must melt   b. don't melt   c. melts

4. If they don't like the art museum, we _____ shopping at a shopping center.

   a. will go   b. went   c. go

H **Look at the pictures and write sentences using *too/enough* as in the example.**

1.

She was too tired, so she couldn't wash the dishes.

→ *She was too tired to wash the dishes.*

2.

Kaitlyn has enough time, so she can go shopping.

→ _____

3.

She is too weak, so she can't carry the suitcase.

→ _____

4.

Dylan is brave enough, so he can go skydiving.

→ _____

I **Read the following sentences. You wish things were different. Write sentences about what you wish.**

1. Your car has broken down, so you have to walk to work.

   → I wish I didn't have to walk to work. _____

2. You want to bake a cake, but you can't remember the recipe.

   → _____

3. You are on a diet, but you want to eat some chocolate.

   → _____

4. You want to go on holiday, but you don't have enough money.

   → _____

J **Agree with Hailey's statements. Write Michael's responses.**

1. I love meeting my friends.

2. I've never been to Seoul.

3. I'll be 12 next month.

4. I'm learning Korean this year.

5. I didn't enjoy the movie.

6. I can speak English very well.

So do I.
_____
_____
_____
_____
_____
_____

You are my
Grammar &
Speaking

3 Student Book

Answer Key

Unit 1

Simple Present vs. Present Progressive   p. 8

Learn & Practice 1

A 2. freezes 3. am sitting / sit

Learn & Practice 2

A 2. is tasting / Action 3. smell / Non-Action
   4. is looking / Action 5. is having / Action
   6. know / Non-action

Learn & Practice 3

A 2. future 3. present 4. present
   5. future 6. future 7. present
   8. present 9. future

Super Writing

A 2. They're going to the concert.
   3. They're playing chess.
   4. She usually eats toast and jam.
B 2. are you going / I'm going with Olivia.
   3. are you meeting / 9 o'clock
   4. Are you going out / I am /
      I'm going to the Italian restaurant.
   5. am meeting Brian at the airport
   6. is he arriving / 8:00
C 3. RIGHT
   4. WRONG / Can you hear those people? What are
      they talking about?
   5. WRONG / Do you believe in God?
   6. WRONG / The government is worried because the
      number of people without jobs is increasing.
D 2. have / having
   3. Do you smell / is smelling
   4. are you thinking / am thinking / Do you like / think

Unit 2

Simple Present vs. Simple Past   p. 14

Learn & Practice 1

A 2. listen / Do you listen to the radio every morning?
   3. sees / Does he see new movies every week?

4. snows / Does it snow a lot in the winter in Korea?
5. broke / Did the Korean War break out in 1950?
6. ate / Did you eat dinner at a family restaurant last
   night?
7. freezes / Does water freeze at zero degrees Celsius?

Learn & Practice 2

A 2. is playing 3. is going
   4. leaves   5. begin
   6. is flying 7. arrives

Learn & Practice 3

A 2. used to brush
   3. used to go
   4. use to ride
   5. didn't use to eat

Super Writing

A 2. Did Cindy play the cello? / No, she didn't. She
      studied Korean.
   3. Does Tara watch a DVD? / No, she doesn't. She
      listens to K-pop music.
   4. Did Aiden go to the movies with his friends? /
      No, he didn't. He visited London.
   5. Did Eric and Susan go to a ballpark to watch a
      baseball game? / No, they didn't. They watched a
      soccer game on TV.
C 3. Isabella used to play badminton after school, but
      she doesn't.
   4. William didn't use to play badminton after school,
      but he does now.
   5. Isabella didn't use to eat lunch at the cafeteria, but
      she does now.
   6. William used to eat lunch at the cafeteria, but he
      doesn't now.
   7. Isabella used to read history books, but she doesn't
      now.
   8. William didn't use to read history books, but he
      does now.
D 2. What time does the baseball game begin tomorrow?
      / The baseball game(It) begins at 5:00 tomorrow.
   3. What time does the laundry shop open tomorrow?
      / The laundry shop(It) opens at 9:00 tomorrow.

Unit 3
Simple Past vs. Past Progressive
p. 20

Learn & Practice 1
A **2.** helped **3.** doing **4.** arrived **5.** was going

Learn & Practice 2
A **2.** was riding / saw
  3. was playing / arrived
  4. went / was brushing
  5. was explaining / fell
  6. was reading / found

Learn & Practice 3
A **2.** We were very surprised when we heard the news. / When we heard the news, we were very surprised.
  3. They started to dance as soon as the music began. / As soon as the music began, they started to dance.

Super Writing
A **2.** Louis was turning the corner when I saw him.
  3. Dana was watching a movie with her father.
  4. While she was driving home, she was listening to her car radio.
  5. The young mothers were holding their babies at the doctor's office.
  6. The girls were having breakfast at the fast food restaurant this morning.
B **2.** What were Katy and Logan doing when you saw them? / They were jogging when I saw them.
  3. What were your parents doing when you came home from school? / They were watching TV when I came home from school.
  4. What was Amanda doing when you came home yesterday? / She was washing her face when I came home yesterday.
C **2.** As soon as the phone rang, I answered it. I answered the phone as soon as it rang.
  3. While I was standing here, the accident occurred. The accident occurred while I was standing here.
  4. When it began to rain, we opened our umbrellas. We opened our umbrellas when it began to rain.
D **2.** arrived / was living **3.** studied
  4. was living / was working **5.** met

6. was living / met **7.** was teaching
8. was teaching / met **9.** was working

Unit 4
The Future Tense
p. 26

Learn & Practice 1
A **2.** is going to **3.** about to **4.** will

Learn & Practice 2
A **2.** will call **3.** go **4.** will pass
B **2.** expands / becomes **3.** doesn't fall / doesn't freeze
  4. go / takes

Learn & Practice 3
A **2.** walk / will go **3.** goes / will spend
  4. visits / will take
B c. - a. - d.

Super Writing
A **2.** She is going to take a trip to Disneyland on Tuesday.
  3. She is going to exercise at the gym on Wednesday.
  4. She is going to visit her grandmother on Thursday.
  5. She is going to go to Ava's farewell party on Friday.
  6. She is going to meet Sandra outside the movie theater at 7:00 on Saturday.
  7. She is going to play badminton with Bob at 10:00 on Sunday.
B **2.** When it's very hot in the summer, plants need lots of water.
  3. If I feel really tired, I (usually) listen to classical music.
  4. When the temperature reaches -15℃, the lake freezes.
C **2.** You won't sleep.
  3. I will take an aspirin and go to bed.
  4. I will buy him a present.
D **2.** If I don't have money, I will get help from the government.
  3. When they go to Seoul next week, they're going to stay at the Hilton Hotel.
E **2.** He is about to wash his hands.
  3. She is about to leave outside.
  4. He is about to take a picture.

Review Test (Unit 1-4)

A 2. usually plays the guitar, but now he is taking swimming lessons.

   3. usually listens to classic music, but now she is riding a skateboard.

   4. usually wash the dishes, but now they are watching a movie.

B 2. present 3. future 4. present 5. future

C 2. didn't use to wear 3. used to watch

D 2. After I got home, I ate dinner. I ate dinner after I got home.

   3. As soon as I heard the doorbell, I opened the door. I opened the door as soon as I heard the doorbell.

E 2. don't have / will get 3. will read / take

   4. visits / will take

F 2. What time does the movie start? / It stars at 9, so we are meeting at the Pizza Hut at 7:30.

   3. What time does Mary arrive? / She arrives at 8, so we are having dinner at 8:30.

G 2. found / was playing

   3. was having / came

   4. were walking / started

H 2. are going to move

   3. will be 4. will give

   5. is going to rain

I 2. c. 3. c. 4. c. 5. c. 6. a.

J 2. Do they love her?

   3. Do you like movies?

   4. Does Susan walk to school?

K 2. is playing

   3. are swimming 4. is reading

L 2. She isn't listening to me.

   3. It isn't raining now.

   4. She isn't wearing a coat.

   5. We aren't enjoying this film.

   6. You aren't eating much these days.

Unit 5
Quantifying Expressions

Learn & Practice 1

A 2. a few 3. little 4. a little 5. few 6. a little

Learn & Practice 2

A 2. much/a lot of 3. much 4. many

   5. many/a lot of 6. much/a lot of

Learn & Practice 3

A 2. a lot of 3. too much 4. too many

   5. a lot of 6. too many 7. too much

Super Writing

A 2. Is there much bread? / No, there is a little bread.

   3. Is there much food? / No, there is little food.

   4. Are there many passengers? / No, there are few passengers.

B 2. If I drink too much coffee, I won't be able to sleep tonight.

   3. There is too much pollution in the big city.

   4. There are too many children in the park today.

   5. The teacher gave us too much homework.

C 2. very little experience 3. very little rain

   4. very few gray whales 5. very little work

   6. Very few countries

D 2. How much bread is there in the basket? / There isn't any bread in the basket.

   3. How many dresses are there in your wardrobe? / There are a lot of dresses in my wardrobe.

   4. How much sugar is there in the fridge? / There isn't any sugar in the fridge.

E 2. There is a little money in my pocket.

   3. There is much sand on his body.

   4. There are a few people at the bus stop.

Unit 6
Expressions of Quantity

Learn & Practice 1

A 2. Most / General 3. Some of / Specific

   4. All of / Specific 5. almost all of / Specific

   6. All / General

Learn & Practice 2

A 2. live 3. are 4. was 5. is 6. have

Learn & Practice 3

A 2. None 3. carries 4. was

   5. None 6. One

Super Writing

A **2.** All of them are wearing skirts. / None of them is/are wearing pants.

3. All of them can swim. / None of them can fly.

4. All of them are expensive. / None of them is/are cheap.

B **2.** Almost all of the students(them)

3. All the students

4. None of the students(them)

5. All the people(students)

6. Some of the students(them)

7. Some of the students(them)

8. None of the students(people)

C **2.** Most of the students in my class are smart and witty.

3. None of the students in my class understand/understands the new math topic.

4. Lotte World is one of my favorite places in the world.

D **3.** Answers will vary.

E **2.** Almost all of the air in the city is polluted.

3. Some of the girls are wearing skirts.

4. None of us can predict the future.

5. One of my favorite movies is *Toy Story*.

6. Almost of all the oceans in the world are polluted.

7. Most of my classmates are always on time for class.

Unit 7
Very, Too, and Enough
p. 48

Learn & Practice 1
A **2.** too

Learn & Practice 2
A **2.** too hot to drink **3.** too tired to finish

4. too expensive to buy **5.** too young to talk

B **2.** for her to eat **3.** for me to wear

4. for us to understand **5.** for me to carry

6. for them to read

Learn & Practice 3
A **2.** hot enough **3.** warm enough

4. enough exercise **5.** good enough

6. enough salt **7.** good enough

8. enough bread

Super Writing

A **2.** is brave enough to go bungee jumping

3. is too hot for the baby to have a bath

4. is too busy to go to the movie theater tonight

B **2.** She can't wear it because it is too big.

3. He can't finish it because he is too sleepy.

4. She can't eat it because it is too hot.

5. She can't wear them because they are too big.

C **2.** The movie was too scary for them to watch.

3. The room was too cold for her to sit in.

4. The magazine is too boring for me to read.

D **2.** My sister was too sleepy to watch the end of the movie on TV.

3. Do you have enough money to buy a T-shirt?

4. We have enough eggs to make an omelet.

E **2.** Answers will vary.

Unit 8
Indefinite Pronouns, One/Ones
p. 54

Learn & Practice 1
A **2.** anything **3.** somebody

4. somewhere **5.** somewhere

6. anything

Learn & Practice 2
A **2.** nothing **3.** nobody(no one)

4. nowhere **5.** nothing

Learn & Practice 3
A **2.** one **3.** one **4.** ones **5.** one

6. one / one **7.** ones

Super Writing

A **2.** anybody / anybody / somebody

3. anywhere / anywhere / somewhere

4. anybody

B **2.** I must get some new ones.

3. I already had one.

4. The one in the car is better.

5. The one on your desk.

6. Can I have a clean one?

C **2.** Somebody **3.** anything **4.** something **5.** anything

6. somebody **7.** anybody

D **2.** There is nobody in the classroom.

3. I have noting to do.

4. She bought nothing yesterday.

5. He told nobody about his plans.

6. There was nobody at home.

E **2.** William doesn't play with anybody at school.

  3. There isn't anything in the desk drawer.

  4. I don't eat anything at night.

  5. We don't have anything for dinner.

  6. There wasn't anybody on the bus.

Review Test (Unit 5–8)
p. 60

A **2.** much **3.** many/a lot of **4.** much

B **2.** a little **3.** a few **4.** little **5.** few

C **2.** Joy isn't energetic enough to go to the party.

  3. Brandon isn't rich enough to buy the house.

D **2.** one **3.** one **4.** ones **5.** ones

E **2.** are **3.** are **4.** study **5.** is

F **2.** One of the students in my class always comes late.

  3. None of the students in this class come/comes from Korea.

G **2.** b. **3.** b.

H **2.** very **3.** too

Unit 9
p. 62

The Passive

Learn & Practice 1

A **2.** was destroyed **3.** loves **4.** helps **5.** is changed

  6. was done

B **2.** was invited **3.** is baked **4.** are taught **5.** is spoken

Learn & Practice 2

A **2.** These toys weren't made by him.

  3. The song wasn't sung by Lady Gaga.

  4. This machine wasn't invented by John.

  5. This book isn't ready by many students.

  6. My wallet wasn't stolen on the bus.

Learn & Practice 3

A **2.** Was the office cleaned? / it wasn't

  3. Was the thief arrested yesterday? / he was

  4. Is English spoken by many people? / it is

5. Were two hundred people employed? / they weren't

Super Writing

A **2.** A lot of rice is eaten in Korea.

  3. Coca-Cola is produced in the USA.

  4. Snails are eaten in France.

B **3.** Rice is grown in Korea.

  4. Is English spoken in Korea?

  5. The mystery was solved by the police.

  6. The trainees are always encouraged by the coach.

  7. This house was built in 1999.

  8. The temple was destroyed in 1900.

  9. Breakfast is usually prepared by Helen.

C **2.** The crayons were invented by Edwin Binney and Harold Smith.

  3. The tea bag was invented by Thomas Sullivan.

  4. The *Harry Potter* books were written by J. K. Rowling.

D **2.** Was the drink invented in 1886 by John Pemberton?

  3. The first McDonald's restaurant was opened by the McDonald brothers.

  4. Are love and understanding needed by all children?

  5. More than 40 million hamburgers are eating every day.

  6. Is soccer played in most countries of the world?

Unit 10
p. 68

Helping Verbs 1

Learn & Practice 1

A **2.** can / can't **3.** Can **4.** Could

Learn & Practice 2

A **2.** Next year I'll be able to ride a bicycle.

  3. They're able to play volleyball.

  4. We weren't able to go on a picnic.

Learn & Practice 3

A **2.** He should stay in bed.

  3. She shouldn't hang out with friends.

  4. She should lose weight.

B **2.** had better not eat **3.** ought to study hard

  4. ought to wash your hands

Learn & Practice 4

A **2.** permission **3.** ability **4.** permission **5.** permission

6. ability

Super Writing

A 4. she could eat with chopsticks

5. she can play badminton

6. she will be able to get a good job

7. she could drink milk

8. she can draw pictures

9. she will be able to meet a boyfriend

10. she could watch TV

11. she can go to a movie

12. she will be able to ride a snowboard

B 2. You can ride a bicycle here.

3. You can cross the road here.

4. You can't use mobile phones here.

5. You can't smoke here.

6. You can have coffee here.

C 2. He had better jog every morning. /
He had better not eat fast food too much.

3. She had better use an alarm clock. /
She had better not go to bed late at night.

D 2. You should eat breakfast every morning.

3. You shouldn't go to bed late every night.

E 2. Dan has a terrible headache. He ought to take an aspirin.

3. I am not able to go ice skating now, but I was able to go ice skating last winter.

4. You ought to brush your teeth after every meal.

5. We aren't able to go mountain climbing now, but we'll be able to go mountain climbing tomorrow.

Unit 11
Helping Verbs 2
p. 74

Learn & Practice 1

A 2. have to study hard 3. Do I have to wear

4. have got to leave 5. had to study

6. Did you have to buy

Learn & Practice 2

A 2. mustn't 3. doesn't have to

4. mustn't / must

Learn & Practice 3

A 2. ability 3. permission 4. possibility

Learn & Practice 4

A 2. can't be 3. must have

Super Writing

A 2. You must be quiet in class.

3. You mustn't tell a lie to your teacher.

4. You must do exercise for your health.

B 3. You mustn't touch pictures in the museum.

4. You don't have to go to school today.

5. You don't have to stay in your seat throughout the flight.

6. You mustn't spend your time playing video games.

7. You don't have to finish your homework tomorrow.

C 2. Does Susan have to go to the grocery store? /
Yes, she does. She has got to get some vegetables.

3. Does Ava has to go shopping? / Yes, she does. She has got to get a new dress.

4. Does Josh have to stay home tonight? /
Yes, he does. He has got to study Korean.

D 2. They must make a lot of money

3. They can't have any children

4. They must like to eat well

E 2. They may not be waiting for us.

3. She could be caught in traffic.

4. She might not be able to find out our house.

Unit 12
Present Perfect 1
p. 80

Learn & Practice 1

A 2. have 3. have 4. have 5. has 6. has

Learn & Practice 2

A 2. have been 3. has finished 4. has rained

5. have eaten 6. has given up

B 2. The students have left.

3. The exams have finished.

4. Steve has broken his leg.

5. She has seen this movie before.

Learn & Practice 3

A 2. hasn't played 3. haven't ridden 4. haven't worked

B 2. Has she seen a ghost? / she hasn't

3. Has Laura lost weight? / she has

4. Have they been here for a long time? / they haven't

Super Writing

A 2. has been a teacher since 2010

   3. have eaten at that restaurant many times

   4. has ridden a horse before

B 2. Have Ryan and Mary traveled by helicopter? /

   No, they haven't. They've traveled by train.

   3. Has Peter lived in France? /

   No, he hasn't. He lived in Korea.

   4. Has Lisa lost her phone? /

   No, she hasn't. She has lost her passport.

C 2. Have Rachel and Ben gone to Europe? /

   No, they haven't.

   3. Has Elizabeth tried bungee jumping? / Yes, she has.

   4. Have Rachel and Ben tried bungee jumping? /

   No, they haven't.

   5. Has Elizabeth seen a scary movie before? /

   No, she hasn't.

   6. Have Rachel and Ben seen a scary movie before? /

   Yes, they have.

D 2. William hasn't ridden an ostrich.

   3. William has read '*War and Peace*'.

   4. William hasn't read '*The Lord of the Rings*'.

   5. William has broken a leg.

   6. William hasn't listened to K-pop music.

   7. William has taken Taekwondo lessons.

   8. William hasn't traveled all over the world.

Review Test (Unit 9–12)

p. 86

A 2. Airplanes were invented by Wright Brothers.

   3. The Eiffel Tower was designed and built by Gustave Eiffel.

   4. *The Last Leaf* was written by O. Henry.

   5. *The Old Man and the Sea* was written by Ernest Hemingway.

   6. *The Mona Lisa* was drawn by Leonardo da Vinci.

B 2. Has Tiffany traveled by airplane? /

   No, she hasn't. She has traveled by train.

C 2. Can I open the window?

   3. May I use the phone (in your office)?

D 2.You mustn't take food

   3. You must pay for your room

   4. You must return to the hotel

   5. You must leave your key

   6. You must leave your room

E 2. Why did he go to the post office yesterday? /

   Because he had to post some letters.

F 2. He had better take a jacket.

   3. You'd better take a taxi.

   4. She'd better not forget her passport.

Unit 13
Present Perfect 2

p. 88

Learn & Practice 1

A 2. since

Learn & Practice 2

A 2. Has Kevin ever worked in an office? /

   Kevin has never worked in an office.

Learn & Practice 3

A 2. been 3. gone 4. been

Learn & Practice 4

A 2. Clara has already eaten dinner.

   3. She has just received a letter from her daughter.

   4. Have they arrived yet?

   5. Has Nicole started her new job yet?

   6. The children have already gone to bed.

   7. He has just bought a new smartphone.

Super Writing

A 2. He has collected stamps for two years.

   3. They have worked for the company since 1999.

   4. It has rained everywhere since last night.

B 3. She hasn't clean the floor yet.

   4. She has already read the magazine.

   5. She hasn't washed the dishes yet.

   6. She has already washed her car.

   7. She hasn't watered the plants yet.

   8. She has already done the shopping.

   9. She has already finished her work.

  10. She hasn't fixed her bicycle yet.

C 2. Have you ever read *War and Peace*? /

   No, I haven't. I have never read *War and Peace*.

   3. Have you ever taken a trip to the Sahara Desert? /

   No, I haven't. I have never taken a trip to the Sahara Desert.

D 2. Jennifer has lived in Seoul for five months.

3. Alan has read two history books since last Monday.

4. They have been married since 2007.

E 2. have / been

   3. has gone to

   4. has been to

Unit 14
Present Perfect 3
p. 94

Learn & Practice 1

A 2. saw 3. made 4. finished

   5. Has Nicole started

Learn & Practice 2

A 2. see 3. has visited 4. have seen 5. had

B 2. went 3. eaten 4. lived 5. have lived

Learn & Practice 3

A 3. was 4. has met 5. worked 6. came

Super Writing

A 2. Have they ever visited Egypt? / Yes, they have. They visited Egypt two months ago.

   3. Have you ever seen the Colosseum? / Yes, I have. I saw it on TV last night.

   4. Have you ever eaten Korean food? / Yes, I have. I ate Korean food yesterday.

   5. Has Jason tried waterskiing? / Yes, he has. He tried waterskiing last month.

   6. Has Mary seen a ghost? / Yes, she has. She saw a ghost yesterday.

B 2. Steve has traveled abroad many times since he started working.

   3. Jenny has lost ten kilos since she joined a health club.

   4. I haven't seen Sheryl since she moved to Australia.

C 3. Bill hasn't prepared for dinner yet.

   4. The man has already repaired our computer. He repaired it on Friday.

   5. My father has already painted our house. He painted it last month.

   6. Olivia and Brian haven't planted any vegetables in their garden yet.

   7. Jennifer has already bought the samrtphone. She bought it last night.

Unit 15
Comparison 1
p. 100

Learn & Practice 1

A 2. from 3. to 4. as 5. different

   6. same 7. similar 8. from

Learn & Practice 2

A 2. bigger than 3. faster than

   4. hotter than 5. more difficult than

   6. more carefully than

   7. better than

Learn & Practice 3

A 2. as tall as 3. not as big as 4. not as healthy as

   5. as well as 6. as cloudy as

Super Writing

A 2. No, she isn't. Jenny is taller than Olivia.

   3. No, she isn't. Jenny is heavier than Olivia.

   4. No, she isn't. Olivia is shorter than Jenny.

   5. No, she isn't. Jenny is older than Olivia.

B 2. City life isn't as easy as village life, but it is more exciting.

   3. The Gyeongbu Expressway isn't as interesting as the country road, but it is faster.

   4. Traveling by plane isn't as cheap as traveling by train, but it is more comfortable.

   5. Compact cars aren't as comfortable as medium-sized passenger cars, but they are easier to park.

C 2. *Avatar* is newer than *Matrix*.

   3. Bill Gates is richer than Barack Obama.

   4. Japan is larger than Korea.

D 2. Days in winter are not longer than days in summer.

   3. The melon is not as small as the apple.

   4. Stuart doesn't speak as slowly as Nick.

E 2. similar 3. similar to 4. the same as

   5. different 6. different from

Unit 16
Comparison 2
p. 106

Learn & Practice 1

A 2. alike 3. like 4. alike 5. like 6. like 7. alike

Learn & Practice 2

A 2. the biggest 3. the most comfortable 4. the tallest
   5. the largest

B 2. of 3. of 4. in

Learn & Practice 3

A 2. one of the best students 3. one of the biggest cities
   4. one of the most popular sites

Super Writing

A 2. The baseball is bigger than the golf ball.
   3. The soccer ball is the biggest of the three.
   4. The golf ball is the smallest of all.

B 2. Hotel B is as old as Hotel D.
   3. Hotel D is older than Hotel C.
   4. Hotel C is newer than Hotel A.
   5. Hotel C is the newest of the four.

C 2. is the most attractive athlete in the world
   3. is one of the most beautiful buildings in the world
   4. is one of the most famous paintings in the world

D 2. Jenny's name is like Jane's name. / Their names are alike.
   3. Carly's car is like Eddie's car. / Their cars are alike.

E 2. I think Russia is the largest country in the world.
   3. I think the cheetah is the fastest animal in the world.
   4. I think cricket is the most popular sport in Australia.

Review Test (Unit 13–16)   p. 112

A 2. I have studied English since I was an elementary school student.
   3. Our teacher has given three tests since the semester began.

B 2. have taken 3. have shopped 4. gave

C 2. Has Aaron every visited Rome? / Yes, he has. He visited Rome five years ago.
   3. Has Jennifer just bought a new telescope? / No, she hasn't. She bought a new digital camera.

D 2. the heaviest 3. heavier than 4. faster than
   5. the smallest 6. as small as

E 2. harder than 3. colder than 4. more crowded than
   5. more expensive than

F 2. Olivia is one of the most intelligent persons in our class.
   3. The Grand Canyon is one of the most beautiful places in the world.
   4. Kim Taehee is one of the prettiest actresses in the world.
   5. The Han River is one of the greatest historical significances of Korea.

Unit 17   p. 114
Gerunds and Infinitives 1

Learn & Practice 1

A 2. Speaking in English
   3. turning on the air conditioner
   4. Swimming in the river
   5. Being on time for school
   6. doing her homework

Learn & Practice 2

A 2. It is very important to study English these days.
   3. It is a good habit to get up early.

Learn & Practice 3

A 2. to do / doing 3. to fight / fighting
   4. to fly / flying

Learn & Practice 4

A 2. for 3. to 4. for

B 2. me to work 3. Jessica to eat
   4. his crew to leave

Super Writing

A 2. Claire called Liam to invite him to her party.
   3. Jason put on his sportswear to go jogging.
   4. He is going to Pizza Hut to have dinner with Eric.

B 2. her(the girl) to use her dictionary
   3. him(the patient) to exercise every day
   4. him(her son) to be careful

C 2. Learning foreign languages is interesting.
   3. Walking alone at night is dangerous.
   4. Watching TV for too long is bad for your eyes.

D 2. wants to see a scary movie
   3. am planning to go to Korea next week
   4. started to talk about her problem

E 2. To learn Korean isn't not difficult.
   3. To get a good job is very hard these days.
   4. To live in a foreign country isn't easy.

F **2.** to play computer games / to learn Japanese
 3. playing computer games / learning Japanese

Unit 18
Gerunds and Infinitives 2
p. 120

Learn & Practice 1
A **2.** going **3.** watching **4.** to learn
B **2.** went camping

Learn & Practice 2
A **2.** I was very delighted to win the lottery.

Learn & Practice 3
A **2.** used to be **3.** is used to driving
 4. is used to doing **5.** used to drink

Learn & Practice 4
A **2.** too cold **3.** too scared **4.** old enough

Super Writing
A **2.** She is strong enough to carry the suitcase.
 3. Dave was too angry to talk to anyone.
 4. She is tall enough to reach the ceiling.
 5. Do you have enough time to go to the park?
 6. They have enough vegetables to make sandwiches.
B **2.** Brittany was ashamed to fail the exam three times.
 3. She was shocked to hear the truth about her boyfriend.
 4. Eric was very happy to buy a new sports car yesterday.
C **2.** learning how to play the guitar
 3. going on holiday tomorrow
 4. being so rude
D **2.** go skiing **3.** goes fishing
E **2.** He is used to sleeping on the floor.
 3. She is used to driving on the right.

Unit 19
Conjunctions
p. 126

Learn & Practice 1
A **2.** and **3.** but **4.** (,) and **5.** , or **6.** but

Learn & Practice 2
A **2.** because **3.** because **4.** , so **5.** because **6.** , so
 7. , so

Learn & Practice 3
A **2.** So am I. **3.** So can I. **4.** Neither will I.

Super Writing
A **2.** They didn't go for a drive because they didn't have time.
 3. It began to rain, so he opened her umbrella.
 4. The weather was cold, but we went fishing anyway.
 5. We can go fishing, or we can just stay home.
B **2.** I don't like salty food, and neither does my wife.
 3. Alex goes to college, and so do his sisters.
 4. Brian can't speak Japanese, and neither can I.
D **2.** but it was closed
 3. because it rained a lot
 4. and watched television
E **2.** I changed my hotel because the rooms were very dirty. / The rooms were very dirty, so I changed my hotel.
 3. He didn't buy the jeans because they were expensive. / The jeans were expensive, so he didn't buy them.
F **2.** So do I. **3.** So did I. **4.** So was I. **5.** Neither will I.
 6. Neither am I.

Unit 20
Conditional Clauses
p. 132

Learn & Practice 1
A **2.** drops / turns

Learn & Practice 2
A **2.** are going to go **3.** may catch

Learn & Practice 3
A **2.** study / first **3.** borrowed / second
 4. were / second **5.** has / first

Learn & Practice 4
A **2.** She wishes her roommate were nice.
 3. She wishes she could go to Korea for her vacation.
 4. She wishes she spoke French.

153

5. She wishes teachers were friendly.

Super Writing

A 2. If we go to Rome, we will see the Colosseum.

3. If we go to New York, we will see the Statue of Liberty.

4. If we go to Sydney, we will see the Sydney Opera House.

5. If we go to Egypt, we will see the Pyramids.

B 2. If I were you, I would wake up earlier in the morning.

3. If I were you, I would apologize to him.

4. If I were you, I would buy her a new one.

C 2. If I get lost when I go to the city center, I use my GPS to find my position.

3. If people are rude and selfish, they don't have many friends.

4. When people recycle plastic bottles, they protect the environment.

D 2. I wish I didn't have a sore throat.

3. I wish I could play outside in the snow.

4. I wish I didn't have to take medicine.

5. I wish I didn't have to stay in bed.

6. I wish I could go to my friend's party tonight.

7. I wish my grandmother were(was) here with me.

4. I wish I had enough money to go on holiday.

J 2. Neither have I. **3.** So will I. **4.** So am I.

5. Neither did I. **6.** So can I.

Review Test (Unit 17–20) p. 138

A 2. used to drink **3.** is used to eating **4.** used to take

5. is used to signing

B 2. I called the hotel desk to ask for an extra pillow.

3. We turned on the radio to listen to the news about the earthquake in Japan.

4. They want to work overtime to earn more money.

C 2. add / floats **3.** throw / pulls **4.** releases / finds

D 2. them to leave now **3.** Jessica to eat her dinner

E 2. My mother was shocked to hear the bad news.

F 2. in watching **3.** for helping **4.** on taking

5. at drawing

G 2. b. **3.** c. **4.** a.

H 2. Kaitlyn has enough time to go shopping.

3. She is too weak to carry the suitcase.

4. Dylan is brave enough to go skydiving.

I 2. I wish I could remember the recipe.

3. I wish I weren't (wasn't) on a diet.